UNVEILING THE MASTERPIECE

DISCOVERING YOUR TRUE IDENTITY AS A YOUNG MAN OF GOD

SCOTT SILVERII

Five
Stones
Press

First Edition

Publisher: Five Stones Press, Dallas, Texas

For quantity sales, textbooks, and orders by trade bookstores or wholesalers contact Five Stones Press at publish@fivestonespress.net

Five Stones Press is owned and operated by Five Stones Church, a nonprofit 501c3 religious organization. Press name and logo are trademarked. Contact publisher for use.

Printed in the United States of America

CONTENTS

All Scripture quotations, unless otherwise indicated, are taken from the New American Standard Bible, ©1960, 1962, 1963, 1968, 1971, 1972, 1973, 1975, 1977, 1995 by The Lockman Foundation. Used by permission.

Other versions used are:

KJV—King James Version. Authorized King James Version.

NIV—Scripture taken from the Holy Bible, New International Version®. Copyright © 1973, 1978, 1984 by International Bible Society. Used by permission of Zondervan Publishing House. All rights reserved.

First Edition

Publisher: Five Stones Press, Dallas, Texas

For quantity sales, textbooks, and orders by trade bookstores or wholesalers contact Five Stones Press at publish@fivestonespress.net

Five Stones Press is owned and operated by Five Stones Church, a nonprofit 501c3 religious organization. Press name and logo are trademarked. Contact publisher for use.

Printed in the United States of America

INTRODUCTION

Welcome, young warrior! Are you ready to embark on an incredible journey of self-discovery and uncover the masterpiece that lies within you? Brace yourselves as you dive into the pages of "Unveiling the Masterpiece: Discovering Your True Identity as a Young Man of God."

In this extraordinary book, we're going to explore what it truly means to be a young man of God. You might be wondering, "Who am I? What is my purpose in this world?" Well, get ready, because we're about to unveil the answers that will ignite your spirit and set your heart ablaze.

You see, you are a masterpiece, intricately designed by the Creator Himself. Inside these pages, you'll embark on a profound journey of self-discovery, unlocking the hidden potential and unique qualities that make you who you are.

Through powerful stories, practical advice, and heartfelt encouragement, you'll learn to embrace your true identity. You'll discover that being a young man of God is not about conforming to society's expectations, but rather, it's about embracing your authentic self and living out your God-given purpose.

We'll delve into important topics that matter to you—building character, navigating friendships, embracing responsibility, and cultivating a strong faith. You'll gain insights and tools to overcome challenges, make wise choices, and develop into the strong, compassionate, and resilient young man that God has called you to be.

This book is a roadmap that will accompany you on your journey of self-discovery. You'll find comfort in knowing that you're not alone on this path—many young men have walked it before you, and their stories will inspire you to rise above any obstacle.

So, young warrior, are you ready to embark on this extraordinary adventure? Are you ready to unveil the masterpiece that lies within you? Get ready to discover your true identity as a young man of God and unleash your potential to impact the world.

Open your heart, turn the page, and let the journey begin. You are a masterpiece in the making, and the world is waiting for you to shine your light. Get ready to uncover the truth, strength, and purpose that are uniquely yours. It's time to unveil the masterpiece that is YOU.

CHAPTER 1
THE CREATOR'S DESIGN FOR YOU

WELCOME to the start of an important topic for your life as a young man growing into an adult child of God. In this chapter, you will explore the incredible truth that God has a specific plan and purpose for your life. You are not a random accident but a deliberate creation of a loving and purposeful God. You will dive into the Bible to understand the foundation of your identity as God's creations and discover the significance and meaning of your existence.

Section 1: Created with Love and Purpose

Have you ever wondered why you are here? Why you exist in this big, wide world? Well, the answer lies in the very beginning. In the Bible, it tells you that God created the heavens, the earth, and everything in them. And guess what?

He created you too! You are not just a random person living at some address on a map. You are part of God's grand design.

In the book of Genesis, it says that God created man and woman in His own image. He formed Adam from the dust of the ground and breathed life into his nostrils. Eve, the first woman, was created from Adam's rib. God took great care and attention in making each and every one of us.

God made you with love and purpose. He didn't make you by accident. He thoughtfully crafted every part of you, from the color of your eyes to the shape of your smile. You are fearfully and wonderfully made, just the way God wanted you to be. Your life is not a mistake; it is a powerful creation with a divine purpose.

The Bible tells you that God has a plan just for you. In the book of Jeremiah, it says, "For I know the plans I have for you, declares the Lord, plans to prosper you and not to harm you, plans to give you hope and a future." Isn't that amazing? God has plans for you that are good and filled with hope. He wants to see you thrive and fulfill your purpose.

Discovering your purpose may take time and patience. It's a journey of seeking God and aligning your heart with His. Spend time in prayer, asking God to reveal His plan for your life. Seek His guidance through reading and studying His Word. As you draw near to God, He will guide your steps and direct your path.

Remember that your purpose is not just about achieving worldly success or gaining recognition. It's about living a life that brings glory to God and blesses others. Your purpose may involve using your talents and passions to serve those in need, sharing the love of Christ, or making a positive impact in your community.

Even when you face challenges or feel uncertain about your purpose, trust that God is with you. In the book of Proverbs, it says, "Trust in the Lord with all your heart, and do not lean on your own understanding. In all your ways acknowledge him, and he will make straight your paths." Lean on God's understanding and trust that He will guide you along the right path.

So, my friend, embrace the truth that you are created with love and purpose. You have a unique role to play in God's greater plan. Seek Him, trust Him, and allow Him to lead you into a life that fulfills your purpose and brings joy and fulfillment. You are a precious creation of God, and He delights in seeing you thrive in the purpose He has designed for you.

Section 2: Made in God's Image

Did you know that you are special? Yes, you! When God created you, He made you in His image. That means you reflect His character and qualities. Just like an artist leaves a bit of themselves in their masterpiece, God put a bit of Himself in you. Isn't that amazing?

In the book of Genesis, it says, "So God created mankind

in his own image, in the image of God he created them; male and female he created them" (Genesis 1:27, NIV). This verse reminds you that you are uniquely designed by God. You carry His imprint within us.

Being made in God's image means that you have the ability to love, to show kindness, and to have a relationship with Him. God is love, and He has given you the capacity to love others just as He loves you. When you extend acts of kindness, forgiveness, and compassion, you mirror God's character.

You have a purpose and a value that goes beyond what you can see or understand. The psalmist writes, "For you created my inmost being; you knit me together in my mother's womb. I praise you because I am fearfully and wonderfully made; your works are wonderful, I know that full well" (Psalm 139:13-14, NIV). God intentionally formed you, and He delights in His creation.

Remember, you are not a mere accident or a random collection of atoms. You are a unique reflection of God's goodness and creativity. Embrace your identity as a child of God, for He has chosen you and has a purpose for your life. Seek to know Him more, to grow in His likeness, and to fulfill the good works He has prepared for you.

As you navigate through challenges, always remember that you are not alone. God, who created you in His image, walks beside you. He understands your struggles, and He is ready to offer His strength and guidance. Place your trust in Him and rely on His unfailing love.

So, embrace your identity as one made in God's image. Cherish the unique qualities and gifts that God has given you. Live your life with purpose, knowing that you have been created for something special. And remember, you are loved beyond measure by the One who made you in His very image.

Section 3: Your Life Has Meaning

Have you ever wondered if your life matters? If you make a difference in this world? Well, let me tell you, it does! God created you for a purpose. He has a plan for your life that is meaningful and significant. You may not always see it or understand it, but trust that God has a good reason for everything He does.

In the Bible, Jeremiah 29:11 says, "For I know the plans I have for you," declares the Lord, "plans to prosper you and not to harm you, plans to give you hope and a future." God's plans for you are good. He wants to see you thrive and fulfill the unique purpose He has designed specifically for you.

Even when life feels confusing or difficult, remember that you are part of a bigger story. You are like a puzzle piece that fits perfectly into God's grand design. Your thoughts, your dreams, your talents—they all have a purpose. Every experience you go through, whether it's joyful or challenging, is shaping you into the person God created you to be.

In the Bible, Ephesians 2:10 reminds us, "For you are God's handiwork, created in Christ Jesus to do good works, which God prepared in advance for us to do." You are God's masterpiece, created with intention and purpose. He has prepared good works for you to do, works that will make a positive impact on the world around you.

Sometimes it's easy to compare yourself to others and feel insignificant. But in God's eyes, you are valuable and irreplaceable. Psalm 139:14 says, "I praise you because I am fearfully and wonderfully made; your works are wonderful, I know that full well." You are fearfully and wonderfully made by the Creator of the universe. Your life has inherent worth and significance.

Even when you face challenges or setbacks, remember that God is with you every step of the way. He promises to never leave you or forsake you (Deuteronomy 31:6). When you feel discouraged, seek strength and guidance from Him. Lean on His promises and trust in His unfailing love.

So, my friend, never doubt the meaning and purpose of your life. You were created by a loving God who has great plans for you. Embrace your uniqueness, seek God's guidance, and step into the purpose He has for you. Your life has meaning, and as you live out your God-given purpose, you will make a difference in this world. Trust in Him and see the incredible impact you can have.

Section 4: Embracing Who You Are

In a world that always tries to tell you who you should be, it's important to remember that your real identity is found in God. When you believe in Jesus and accept Him as your Savior, you become part of God's family. You become His children, and that's who you truly are. The Bible tells you in John 1:12, "But to all who did receive him, who believed in his name, he gave the right to become children of God."

Your worth and value don't come from your achievements, popularity, or things you own. They come from God's love, forgiveness, and choosing us. No matter what mistakes you've made in the past, God's love for you stays strong and unconditional. Psalm 103:17 says, "But from everlasting to everlasting the Lord's love is with those who fear him, and his righteousness with their children's children."

You don't need to try hard to be accepted or approved by the world. God has already established your worth. Ephesians 1:4-5 reminds you, "Even before he made the world, God loved you and chose us in Christ to be holy and without fault in his eyes. God decided in advance to adopt us into his own family by bringing us to himself through Jesus Christ. This is what he wanted to do, and it gave him great pleasure."

When you embrace your identity as God's children, you can find security, peace, and a sense of purpose. You can let go of the pressure to be like everyone else and instead live according to God's truth. You can find your value in simply being who God created you to be.

So, let's not let others or your own doubts define who you are. Let's embrace your identity as God's children and let His truth determine your worth. As you live out your identity in Christ, you can experience the fullness of God's love and confidently follow the purpose He has for you.

Section 5: Living Free and True

Living free is a wonderful gift that God has given us. In Galatians 5:1, the Bible says, "It is for freedom that Christ has set us free." This freedom isn't just a temporary feeling but a deep truth that shapes your lives.

When you understand who you are in Christ, you no longer have to be trapped by your past mistakes. In Psalm 103:12, it says, "As far as the east is from the west, so far has he removed your transgressions from us." God's forgiveness is complete and unconditional. He doesn't hold your past mistakes against us, and you shouldn't either. You can let go of guilt and shame, knowing that God has wiped away your sins.

Living free also means breaking free from what others think or say about us. In Romans 8:1, it says, "Therefore, there is now no condemnation for those who are in Christ Jesus." When you find your identity in Christ, you don't need to seek approval from others. You can find your worth and value in

Him alone. You can be true to yourself , embracing who God made you to be.

Fear and insecurity can hold you back from fully living in the freedom Christ has given us. But in 2 Timothy 1:7, it says, "For God has not given us a spirit of fear, but of power and of love and of a sound mind." You can let go of fear and boldly step forward in faith. You can pursue your passions and dreams, knowing that God has given you unique gifts and abilities.

Comparing yourself to others is another trap that steals your freedom. In Galatians 6:4, it says, "Each one should test their own actions. Then they can take pride in themselves alone, without comparing themselves to someone else." God has created you uniquely, with a purpose and a calling. When you compare yourself to others, you miss out on appreciating your own journey. Let's celebrate the strengths and successes of others while embracing your own God-given identity.

Living free means shining brightly for God's glory. In Matthew 5:14-16, it says, "You are the light of the world... Let your light shine before others, that they may see your good deeds and glorify your Father in heaven." you are called to live in a way that reflects God's love and goodness. When you embrace your identity in Christ, you can live boldly and impact the world around you with His love.

Living free means understanding your identity in Christ and embracing the truth that you have been set free. You can let go of your past, break free from the opinions of others, and overcome fear and insecurity. You don't have to compare yourself to others because you are uniquely created by God. Let's live fully as who God made you to be and shine brightly for His glory.

Section 6: Growing Closer to God

To understand God's plan for your life, it's important to develop a stronger relationship with Him. Just like any friendship, it takes time and effort. God wants to be by your side every step of the way and show you His plan for your life.

The Bible, which is God's Word, is like a helpful guidebook for life. It is filled with wisdom and truth. Make it a habit to read and study the Bible regularly. As you explore its pages, you will learn about God's character, His promises, and His instructions for living a meaningful and purposeful life. The more you immerse yourself in the Bible, the clearer God's plan for your life will become.

Prayer is another important part of growing closer to God. It is a way to talk to Him and express your thoughts, desires, and concerns. Set aside time each day to have a conversation with God and listen for His guidance. Sometimes, He may speak to you through the Bible, where you might find verses that directly apply to your situation. He may also speak to your heart, giving you peace and guiding you in the decisions you need to make.

Seeking wisdom and guidance from God is crucial.

Proverbs 3:5-6 says, "Trust in the Lord with all your heart and do not rely on your own understanding; in all your ways submit to him, and he will make your paths straight." When you face decisions, seek His advice and trust that He will guide you in the right direction. He may use godly mentors or wise friends to offer you advice and support.

Growing closer to God is a journey that requires commitment and dedication. It's not always easy, and there may be times when you feel far away from Him or struggle to understand His plan. However, remember that God is always faithful. He wants a close relationship with you and will reveal His plan for your life at the perfect time.

As you spend time with God, you will develop a deeper understanding of His character and His love for you. You will begin to align your desires with His desires and find joy and fulfillment in following His plan. Trust that God's plan for your life is unique and made specifically for you. Embrace the process of growing closer to Him, knowing that as you draw nearer to God, He will guide you into the abundant life He has prepared for you.

Section 7: Trusting in God's Guidance

Trusting in God's guidance is an important part of overcoming challenges and staying strong in your faith. The Bible is full of verses that assure you of God's faithfulness and His desire to lead you in the right direction. In the book of

Proverbs, it says, "Trust in the Lord with all your heart and do not rely on your own understanding; in all your ways submit to him, and he will make your paths straight" (Proverbs 3:5-6).

When you trust in God, you acknowledge that He is wiser than you are. You understand that His plans for your life are greater than anything you could imagine. With that understanding, know that God has the best for you.

Trusting in God's guidance doesn't mean that everything will always go smoothly or according to your wishes. There may be times when you face challenges or unexpected detours along the way. However, you can take comfort in knowing that God is always with you on your journey. As the psalmist David assures you in Psalm 32:8, "I will instruct you and teach you in the way you should go; I will counsel you with my loving eye on you."

Even in moments when you are unsure or confused, you can trust that God's intentions for your life are good. He sees the bigger picture while you can only see a small part. The Apostle Paul reminds you in Romans 8:28, "And you know that in all things God works for the good of those who love him, who have been called according to his purpose." This verse reassures you that even when things don't go as you planned, God is working behind the scenes for your ultimate benefit.

Trusting in God's guidance means surrendering your own understanding and seeking His will above your own. It involves letting go of your worries and anxieties and placing them in His capable hands. As you release control and rest in His sovereignty, you can experience a peace that goes beyond your understanding (Philippians 4:7).

Remember, you are never alone on your journey. God is always there, ready to guide you and lead you in the right direction. Trust in Him, rely on His promises, and depend on His guidance. As you put your faith in God's hands, you will find the strength to overcome challenges, remain firm in your faith, and confidently step into the future He has planned for you.

Section 8: Embracing Your Unique Calling

God has created you with unique gifts, talents, and passions. It's important to take the time to discover and embrace the calling that God has placed on your life. Your calling is the specific purpose and mission that God has for you. It may not look the same as someone else's, and that's perfectly fine.

In 1 Corinthians 12:4-6, it says, "There are different kinds of gifts, but the same Spirit distributes them. There are different kinds of service, but the same Lord. There are different kinds of working, but in all of them and in everyone it is the same God at work." This passage assures you that your diverse gifts and callings are all part of God's grand plan.

To embrace your unique calling, start by reflecting on what truly inspires and excites you. What activities or causes make your heart come alive? These passions and interests could be indications of the calling that God has placed on your life. Pray and ask God to reveal His plan to you. Seek His guidance through His Word, the Bible, and listen to the promptings of the Holy Spirit.

It's important to remember that your calling is not about comparing yourself to others or trying to fit into someone else's mold. In Galatians 6:4, it says, "Each one should test their own actions. Then they can take pride in themselves alone, without comparing themselves to someone else." God has designed you uniquely, with your own set of talents and abilities. Embrace who you are and trust that God will guide you as you walk in obedience to Him.

As you step into your unique calling, there may be challenges and obstacles along the way. But remember, God equips those He calls. In Philippians 4:13, it says, "I can do all this through him who gives me strength." With God's strength and guidance, you can fulfill your calling and make a positive impact on the world around you.

Embracing your unique calling is an exciting and fulfilling journey. It may lead you to different places, open new doors, and touch the lives of others. Trust in God's plan for your life, lean on His strength, and be willing to step out in faith. As you walk in alignment with your calling, you will experience the joy and fulfillment that comes from living out the purpose for which you were created.

Section 9: Overcoming Doubts and Obstacles

Discovering and pursuing your God-given mission may not always be smooth sailing. Doubts and obstacles can arise along the way, causing you to question your abilities and the validity of your calling. However, it's essential to remember that God equips those He calls. He will provide everything you need to fulfill His plan for your life.

In the Bible, you see numerous examples of individuals who faced doubts and obstacles but ultimately overcame them with God's help. Moses doubted his ability to lead the Israelites out of Egypt, but God assured him of His presence and provided signs and wonders to demonstrate His power (Exodus 3-4). Gideon questioned his ability to deliver Israel from the Midianites, but God assured him of His presence and gave him the strength to accomplish the task (Judges 6-8).

When doubts arise, turn to God's Word for encouragement and seek the support of fellow believers. The Bible is filled with promises and stories of God's faithfulness. Meditate on verses such as Philippians 4:13, which says, "I can do all things through Christ who strengthens me." Remind yourself that God has a purpose for your life, and He will guide you every step of the way.

Surround yourself with a community that believes in your calling and can provide guidance and accountability. Seek out mentors or spiritual leaders who can offer wisdom and support. Share your doubts and concerns with them, allowing them to speak truth and encouragement into your life. Remember that God often uses other believers to confirm and affirm His calling on your life.

During moments of doubt, take time to pray and seek God's guidance. Ask Him to reveal His plan and purpose for your life. Trust in His timing and His ability to overcome any obstacle that stands in your way. Remember the words of Jesus in Matthew 19:26, "With man, this is impossible, but with God all things are possible."

In moments of doubt, remind yourself of God's faithfulness throughout history and in your own life. Reflect on past instances where God has provided, protected, and guided you. Use these experiences as reminders of His unwavering love and care.

As you face obstacles, remember that they can be opportunities for growth and refinement. God often uses challenges to strengthen your faith and mold you into the person He created you to be. Embrace the process, knowing that God is working all things together for your good (Romans 8:28).

Please remember that doubts and obstacles are a normal part of the journey towards fulfilling your God-given mission. Trust in God's equipping, seek support from the Word and fellow believers, and rely on His guidance and strength. Remember the examples of faith from the Bible and the promises of God's faithfulness. With God by your side, you can overcome any doubt or obstacle that comes your way.

Section 10: Taking Action and Making an Impact

Taking action and making an impact is an essential part of living out your God-given mission. In the Bible, James 2:17 reminds you that faith without works is dead. It's not enough to simply believe in God and understand your identity in Him; you must also put your faith into action.

Look for opportunities to serve others just as Jesus did. In Mark 10:45, Jesus said, "For even the Son of Man came not to be served but to serve, and to give his life as a ransom for many." Jesus set an example for you by humbly serving others, and you are called to follow in His footsteps.

Take a moment to reflect on your unique gifts and talents. In 1 Peter 4:10, it says, "Each of you should use whatever gift you have received to serve others, as faithful stewards of God's grace in its various forms." God has given you specific abilities for a reason—to bless others and bring glory to Him.

Start by looking within your community for opportunities to serve. Is there a local shelter or food pantry where you can volunteer your time? Can you use your skills in music, art, or writing to bring joy and inspiration to those who need it? Seek out ways to make a difference in the lives of those around you.

Remember, you don't have to wait for the perfect moment to start. God can use you right where you are. In Exodus 4:2, God asked Moses, "What is that in your hand?" Similarly, God wants to use what you already have in your hands to make an impact. It could be your time, resources, or even a kind word to encourage someone who is struggling.

Trust in God's guidance as you take action. Proverbs 3:5-6 says, "Trust in the LORD with all your heart, and do not lean on your own understanding. In all your ways acknowledge him, and he will make straight your paths." As you step out in faith, God will lead and direct your steps.

Remember that even small acts of kindness can have a ripple effect. A smile, a listening ear, or a helping hand can brighten someone's day and show them the love of Christ. Your actions can be a reflection of God's love and bring hope to those who are hurting.

Finally, don't underestimate the impact you can make in the lives of others. Take action, serve with humility, and trust in God's guidance. As you use your unique gifts and talents, you can be a light in a dark world and bring glory to His name. Let your actions speak of your faith and be a testament to the transforming power of God's love.

Wrap Up

Understanding God's plan for your life starts with recognizing that you are not an accident. You are a deliberate creation of a loving and purposeful God. Embrace your identity as a child of God, knowing that your life has meaning and significance. Seek a growing relationship with Him, trusting in His guidance and living in the freedom that comes from knowing who you are in Christ. Remember, you are a masterpiece in the hands of the Creator, and He has a beautiful plan for your life.

Stepping into your God-given identity is an exciting and fulfilling journey. By embracing your unique calling, overcoming doubts and obstacles, taking action, persevering in God's promises, and leaving a lasting legacy, you can make a significant impact on the world around you. Trust in God's guidance, rely on His strength, and follow His leading as you step into the purpose for which you were created. Remember, with God by your side, you have the power to impact the world and bring glory to His name.

CHAPTER 2
MASTERPIECE IN THE MAKING: EMBRACING YOUR UNIQUENESS

EMBRACING your uniqueness as a masterpiece in the making is the foundation of understanding how amazing you are. God created you with specific talents, strengths, and characteristics that make you one-of-a-kind. Let's delve into the journey of discovering and embracing your uniqueness.

Section 1: Created with Purpose

Did you know that God made you for a reason? You're not just a random person with no purpose. God created you with a plan in mind. He designed you with special talents and abilities that He wants to use for something great. You have a unique purpose that only you can fulfill.

Think about it for a moment. God, the Creator of the universe, took the time to form you. He shaped every part of you, from your appearance to your personality. He gave you specific talents and passions that make you who you are. You are fearfully and wonderfully made.

God didn't just create you for the sake of it. He has a purpose for your life. He wants to use you to bring glory to Him and to make a positive impact in the world around you. You may not know exactly what that purpose is yet but rest assured that God has a plan for you.

Discovering your purpose begins with seeking God. Spend time in prayer and ask Him to reveal His plan for your life. Seek His guidance and listen to His voice. He may speak to you through His Word, through the counsel of others, or through the stirring in your heart. Trust that He will lead you in the right direction.

Your purpose is not limited to a specific career or role. It's about living a life that honors God and serves others. Your purpose may involve using your talents to bless those around you, whether it's through acts of kindness, sharing your knowledge, or using your creativity. Your purpose may be to be a loving spouse, a caring parent, a faithful friend, or a dedicated employee.

Don't compare yourself to others or feel discouraged if you haven't figured out your purpose yet. Remember that God's timing is perfect, and He will reveal His plan for you in due time. Focus on developing your relationship with Him and being faithful with what He has given you now. Your purpose will unfold as you walk with Him step by step.

Embrace the truth that you are valuable and significant. You are not a mistake or an accident. You are created with purpose. Your life has meaning, and God wants to use you to make a difference. Trust in His plan and be open to the opportunities He brings your way. Don't be afraid to step out in faith and pursue your passions, knowing that God is with you every step of the way.

So, remember, you are not here by chance. You were intentionally created by a loving God with a unique purpose in mind. Seek Him, trust Him, and allow Him to guide you on the incredible journey of discovering and fulfilling your purpose. Your life has a greater significance than you can imagine, and with God's help, you can make a lasting impact in this world.

Section 2: Unraveling the Lies of Comparison

In a world where social media dominates your lives, it's hard not to get caught up in the trap of comparison. You scroll through carefully curated profiles, envy the seemingly perfect lives of others, and start questioning your own worth. But let me tell you something: comparison is a lie that can rob you of joy and hinder your understanding of God's purpose for your life.

Here's the truth: God created you to be uniquely you. He designed every aspect of your being, from your appearance to your personality, with intention and purpose. You are fearfully and wonderfully made, and there is no one else in the world like you. So why waste your time comparing yourself to others?

Comparison is a never-ending cycle that leads to discontentment and self-doubt. When you constantly measure yourself against others, you'll always find someone who seems better, prettier, smarter, or more successful than you. But here's the secret: those comparisons are often based on superficial and incomplete information.

Social media, for example, only shows a carefully curated highlight reel of people's lives. Behind the filtered photos and perfectly crafted captions, there are struggles, insecurities, and imperfections that are rarely shared. Remember that what you see online is just a glimpse into someone's life, not the whole picture.

Instead of comparing yourself to others, focus on embracing your uniqueness. God has given you a set of talents, passions, and experiences that make you one of a kind. Your role in this world is specific to you, and no one else can fulfill it. Embrace your strengths and work on improving your weaknesses, but do it for your own growth, not to outshine someone else.

When you let go of comparison, you free yourself from the burden of trying to meet unrealistic standards. You can start appreciating your own journey and the progress you're making. Remember, life is not a competition. It's about becoming the best version of yourself and fulfilling the purpose God has for you.

Instead of comparing yourself to others, celebrate their successes. Learn to genuinely rejoice with those who achieve their goals and accomplishments. Cultivate a heart of gratitude for the blessings in your own life. When you shift your focus from comparison to gratitude, you'll find greater contentment and joy.

If you find yourself slipping back into the comparison trap, take a step back and refocus on what truly matters. Spend time in prayer and meditate on God's Word. Seek His guidance and ask Him to reveal the unique path He has for you. Trust that He has a plan for your life that is tailor-made for you.

Remember, you are fearfully and wonderfully made. God's love for you is unconditional and not based on comparison. Embrace your uniqueness, celebrate the journey, and trust that God's plan for your life is far greater than anything you could ever imagine. Step out of the shadow of comparison and into the light of your God-given purpose.

Section 3: Discovering Your Strengths

Take some time to explore and discover your strengths. It's important to recognize the unique talents and abilities that God has given you. What are you naturally good at? What activities bring you joy and fulfillment? God has equipped you with these strengths for a reason, and when you use them, you can make a positive impact in the world.

Start by reflecting on the things that come easily to you or the activities that you excel in. Maybe you have a knack for problem-solving, artistic skills, or the ability to connect with others. Pay attention to the activities that bring you joy and a sense of fulfillment. These can be clues to your strengths.

You can also seek feedback from others who know you well. Ask your friends, family, or mentors what they see as your strengths. Sometimes, others can see qualities in you that you may not recognize in yourself .

Once you have identified your strengths, think about how you can use them to serve others and make a difference. For example, if you're a good listener, you can offer a listening ear to those who are struggling. If you have leadership skills, you can take on roles that allow you to guide and inspire others.

Remember that your strengths may evolve and develop over time. Be open to learning new skills and growing in areas where you have potential. Embrace a growth mindset that believes in your ability to learn and improve.

By discovering and embracing your strengths, you align yourself with God's plan for your life. You become more confident in who you are and what you have to offer. Your strengths are not just for your benefit but also for the betterment of those around you. So, take the time to explore and nurture your strengths, and watch as they become powerful tools for impacting the world and fulfilling your God-given mission.

Section 4: God Loves Diversity.

Just look at the world around you – the countless species of animals, the variety of flowers, and the uniqueness of each person. God didn't create clones; He created individuals. Embrace your individuality and celebrate the fact that you are wonderfully different from anyone else.

In a world that often pressures you to conform and fit into molds, it's important to remember that God intentionally made you unique. He designed you with specific talents, passions, and characteristics that set you apart. Your individuality is not a mistake or a flaw; it's a beautiful reflection of God's creativity.

When you embrace your individuality, you tap into your God-given potential. You discover the strengths and talents that make you who you are. Don't compare yourself to others or try to be someone you're not. Instead, focus on being the best version of yourself.

Embracing your individuality also means accepting and loving yourself. It's about recognizing your worth and value as a child of God. You are fearfully and wonderfully made, and there is no one else like you in the world. So, embrace your quirks, embrace your passions, and embrace your unique perspective on life.

When you fully embrace your individuality, you can make a significant impact on the world around you. Your unique perspective and gifts can contribute to solving problems, bringing about change, and making a difference. Don't be afraid to think outside the box, take risks, and share your ideas with others.

Remember, God has a purpose for your life that is intricately tied to your individuality. He has a plan that only you can fulfill. So, embrace who you are and trust that God will use your uniqueness to bring glory to His name and bless those around you.

In a world that often values conformity, be a shining example of embracing individuality. Show others that it's okay to be different, to think differently, and to pursue their own God-given path. Encourage others to celebrate their individuality and support them in their journey of self-discovery.

As you embrace your individuality, remember to seek God's guidance, and align your life with His will. Your individuality should be an expression of your relationship with Him and a way to honor and serve Him. Trust that He will continue to mold and shape you into the person He created you to be.

So, embrace your individuality. Embrace the unique person God made you to be. Celebrate your differences and use them to impact the world. You have a special role to play in God's grand design, and your individuality is an essential part of that. Embrace it with joy and confidence and watch as God uses you to make a beautiful and lasting impact on the world.

Section 5: Overcoming the Fear of Standing Out

It's natural to feel afraid of standing out or being different from those around us. You may worry about judgment, rejection, or not fitting in. But as Christians, you are called to be set apart and shine your light for God. In the Bible, Jesus tells you in Matthew 5:14-16, "You are the light of the world... let your light shine before others, that they may see your good deeds and glorify your Father in heaven."

God created you uniquely, with your own gifts, talents, and personalities. He wants you to embrace your individuality and use it to make a positive impact in the world. Just like the various parts of a body work together harmoniously, you are all important and necessary for God's purposes (1 Corinthians 12:12-27).

When you let fear hold you back, you limit your potential and hinder God's plans for your lives. Remember the story of David, a young shepherd boy who stood out by defeating the giant Goliath. Despite the odds against him, David trusted in God's strength and stepped forward courageously (1 Samuel 17). He didn't allow fear to stop him from fulfilling his destiny.

To overcome the fear of standing out, you must shift your

focus from seeking the approval of others to seeking God's approval. He is the one who created you and knows you intimately. Psalm 139:14 reminds you that you are fearfully and wonderfully made by God. You can find comfort and confidence in knowing that you are loved and accepted by your Heavenly Father just as you are.

It's also important to surround yourself with a supportive Christian community. Find like-minded individuals who will encourage and uplift you in your journey. Together, you can spur one another on to embrace your unique identities and fulfill God's calling for your life (Hebrews 10:24-25).

When you feel the fear of standing out creeping in, take a moment to pray and ask God for strength and boldness. Remember the promise found in Isaiah 41:10, "So do not fear, for I am with you; do not be dismayed, for I am your God. I will strengthen you and help you; I will uphold you with my righteous right hand."

As you step out in faith, you may encounter challenges or face opposition, but God will equip you with everything you need. He will guide and empower you to fulfill your purpose. Trust in His plan, lean on His promises, and allow His love to cast out all fear (1 John 4:18).

Embracing your uniqueness and standing out may inspire others to do the same. You never know the impact you can have on someone's life by simply being true to who God created you to be. By shining your light brightly, you glorify

God and become a beacon of hope and encouragement to those around you.

So, let go of the fear of standing out. Embrace your uniqueness and trust in God's plan for your life. Step forward boldly, knowing that you are called to make a difference in this world. You are fearfully and wonderfully made, and your light has the power to illuminate the darkness.

Section 6: Using Your Talents for God's Glory

Your talents and abilities are not just for personal gain; they are meant to be used for God's glory and the benefit of others. Think about the talents and abilities that God has given you. Are you good at playing an instrument, writing, painting, or working with your hands? Maybe you have a talent for organizing or leading others. Whatever it may be, remember that these gifts are not by chance but are God-given.

When you use your talents for God's glory, you bring Him honor and reflect His love to the world. Your talents can be a means of showing kindness and compassion to others. For example, if you are good at playing an instrument, you can use your music to bring comfort and joy to those who are hurting. If you have a talent for writing, you can use your words to inspire and encourage others.

Jesus taught you in Matthew 5:16, "In the same way, let your light shine before others, that they may see your good deeds and glorify your Father in heaven." When you use your talents to serve others, you become a shining light that points people to God.

It's important to remember that using your talents for God's glory doesn't mean seeking recognition or praise for yourself. Instead, it's about acknowledging that your abilities come from God and using them to bless others selflessly.

You can start by seeking opportunities in your church, community, or even among your family and friends. Volunteer your time and talents to help those in need. Use your skills to make a positive impact, whether it's by teaching others, creating something beautiful, or simply lending a helping hand.

As you use your talents for God's glory, remember that it's not about being the best or most talented. God values your willingness to serve and the heart behind your actions. 1 Corinthians 10:31 reminds us, "So whether you eat or drink or whatever you do, do it all for the glory of God."

God has uniquely gifted you, and when you use your talents to serve others, you participate in His plan to bring love, hope, and transformation to the world. So, embrace your uniqueness, seek opportunities to use your gifts, and let your talents be a channel of God's love for the benefit of others. By doing so, you not only bring glory to God but also experience the joy and fulfillment that comes from living out your purpose.

Section 7: Embracing Growth and Improvement

Embracing your uniqueness doesn't mean that you stop growing or improving. God wants you to continually develop and enhance your gifts and talents. He desires to see you flourish and make the most of the potential He has placed within you. Just as a plant needs water and sunlight to grow, you need nourishment and opportunities to grow in your relationship with God and in your abilities.

In the Bible, you find numerous examples of individuals who embraced growth and improvement. King Solomon, known for his wisdom, asked God for understanding and knowledge, and God granted his request (1 Kings 3:9). The apostle Paul encouraged the early Christians to "grow in the grace and knowledge of your Lord and Savior Jesus Christ" (2 Peter 3:18). These examples remind you of the importance of actively seeking growth in your lives.

To embrace growth and improvement, be intentional about investing time and effort into your personal development. Set goals that align with God's purposes for your life. It could be improving your communication skills, deepening your understanding of the Bible, or developing leadership qualities. Seek out mentors and role models who can guide and inspire you. Surround yourself with people who challenge you to be better and hold you accountable.

Remember, growth is not always easy. It often requires stepping out of your comfort zone and embracing new challenges. But trust that God will equip you with what you need. As the apostle Paul wrote, "I can do all things through Christ who strengthens me" (Philippians 4:13). Lean on His strength and guidance as you embark on your journey of growth.

Additionally, embrace a mindset of continuous improvement. Celebrate your successes, but also learn from your failures and setbacks. They are opportunities for growth and learning. Allow God to refine and mold you, knowing that He is constantly working on your character and transforming you into the image of Christ.

As you embrace growth and improvement, remember to seek God's wisdom and direction. Pray for His guidance and ask Him to reveal areas in your life that need growth. He will lead you on a path of personal transformation and use your growth to impact the world around you.

Embracing growth and improvement is a vital aspect of understanding your identity in God. As you develop and enhance your gifts and talents, you align yourself with His purposes and contribute to His kingdom. Embrace growth with a humble and teachable spirit, seeking God's guidance and relying on His strength. Trust that He will continue to shape you into the person He has created you to be. Embrace the journey of growth and improvement, knowing that God is with you every step of the way.

Section 8: Supporting Others in Their Uniqueness

In the Bible, you are reminded of the importance of supporting and uplifting one another. Romans 12:10 encourages you to "Love one another with brotherly affection. Outdo one another in showing honor." When you support others in their uniqueness, you are living out this commandment.

God has created each person with unique gifts, talents, and abilities. Just as He has shaped you for a specific purpose, He has also designed others with their own unique calling. It is your role as Christians to recognize and appreciate the diversity within the body of Christ.

When you encounter someone who possesses different strengths or talents than your own, resist the temptation to feel insecure or envious. Instead, choose to celebrate their uniqueness. Encourage them in their journey, affirm their abilities, and cheer them on as they pursue God's calling in their lives.

Proverbs 27:17 tells us, "As iron sharpens iron, so one person sharpens another." By supporting and uplifting others, you sharpen each other's skills and character. You can learn from one another, draw inspiration, and grow together in your faith.

In 1 Thessalonians 5:11, the Apostle Paul urges believers to "encourage one another and build one another up." When you support others in their uniqueness, you are actively participating in this call to encourage and uplift one another. You become a source of strength and motivation for those around us.

Remember that supporting others does not diminish your own worth or calling. Instead, it strengthens the body of Christ as you work together in unity. Each person's uniqueness contributes to the rich tapestry of God's kingdom.

As you interact with others, be intentional about creating an environment of acceptance and appreciation. Encourage them to embrace their unique gifts and talents and remind them that they are fearfully and wonderfully made (Psalm 139:14). Celebrate their successes and offer a helping hand when they face challenges.

In Galatians 6:2, you are instructed to "Bear one another's burdens, and so fulfill the law of Christ." Supporting others means being there for them in both joyful and difficult times. It means listening, offering guidance, and providing a safe space where they can express themselves without judgment.

Ultimately, supporting others in their uniqueness reflects the love of Christ. Jesus Himself demonstrated this love by valuing and uplifting those around Him. Follow His example and extend grace, encouragement, and support to others as they navigate their own journeys of faith.

Section 9: Cultivating Self-Acceptance and Confidence

Embracing your uniqueness requires cultivating self-acceptance and confidence. It's important to understand that you are fearfully and wonderfully made by God, as the Bible tells you in Psalm 139:14. God created you with intention and purpose, and He loves you just the way you are.

To cultivate self-acceptance, it's essential to embrace all aspects of yourself. Recognize that you have strengths, weaknesses, and quirks. None of us are perfect, and that's okay. Acceptance means embracing your authentic self, including your imperfections. Remember that God's grace is sufficient for you, as stated in 2 Corinthians 12:9. His love and acceptance of you are unconditional.

Building confidence starts with focusing on your positive qualities and achievements. Instead of dwelling on your flaws or comparing yourself to others, celebrate the unique gifts and talents God has given you. Philippians 4:13 reminds you that you can do all things through Christ who strengthens us. With God's help, you can overcome challenges and accomplish great things.

Take time to reflect on how God has worked in your life in the past. Recall moments when He provided guidance, protection, and blessings. These reminders can boost your confidence in His faithfulness and provision for your future.

Prayer is a powerful tool for cultivating self-acceptance and confidence. Take your fears, insecurities, and doubts to

God in prayer. Ask Him to help you see yourself through His eyes and to believe in the unique purpose He has for your life. Seek His guidance and trust that He will equip you for whatever lies ahead.

Surround yourself with a supportive community of believers who can encourage and affirm your worth. Romans 12:4-5 reminds you that you are all members of one body in Christ, and you can uplift and support one another. Seek out mentors and friends who can speak truth into your life and remind you of your value in God's eyes.

Remember, cultivating self-acceptance and confidence is a journey. It takes time and intentional effort. But as you embrace who you are, trust in God's plan, and rely on His strength, you will grow in self-acceptance and confidence. You are a unique creation of God, and He has great things in store for you. Walk in the assurance of His love and embrace your identity as a beloved child of God.

Section 10: Finding Your Niche

Discovering your niche is a crucial step in embracing your uniqueness. It's about finding the areas where your passion and abilities intersect. God designed you with specific talents and gifts. The Bible tells you in Psalm 139:14, "I praise you because I am fearfully and wonderfully made." God has designed you with purpose and intention.

Take time to reflect on what makes you come alive. What

activities or causes ignite a fire within you? What are you naturally good at? Seek God's guidance and ask Him to reveal your niche. He knows you better than anyone else and wants to guide you towards fulfilling your God-given purpose.

When you discover your niche, you can make a significant impact in that particular area. It could be in a specific field, profession, or area of service. God has equipped you with unique strengths and passions to shine in that space. The apostle Paul reminds you in 1 Corinthians 12:4-6, "Now there are varieties of gifts, but the same Spirit; and there are varieties of service, but the same Lord."

By embracing your niche, you can bring glory to God and contribute to His kingdom. Whether you excel in art, leadership, teaching, technology, or any other field, use your talents to serve others and make a positive impact. The Bible encourages you in 1 Peter 4:10, "As each has received a gift, use it to serve one another, as good stewards of God's varied grace."

Finding your niche is not about seeking personal success or recognition. It's about aligning your unique abilities with God's purpose for your life. It's about using your talents to bring light to dark places and bring hope to those in need. When you operate in your niche, you become a vessel through which God's love and grace can flow.

Remember, finding your niche may require exploration and stepping out of your comfort zone. It's a journey of self-discovery and reliance on God's guidance. Be open to new experiences and opportunities that may lead you to your niche. Trust that God will lead you to where you can make the most impact for His kingdom.

As you discover and embrace your niche, stay connected to God through prayer and regular study of His Word. Seek His wisdom and guidance in all that you do. Proverbs 3:6 reminds us, "In all your ways acknowledge him, and he will make straight your paths." Trust that He will direct your steps and use your unique gifts for His glory.

Finding your niche is an important part of embracing your uniqueness and making a significant impact in the world. Discover where your passion and abilities intersect and seek God's guidance in identifying your niche. Use your talents to serve others and bring glory to God. Remember, it's not about personal success but about aligning your unique gifts with God's purpose for your life. Step out in faith, trusting that God will lead you to where you can shine the brightest.

Wrap Up

You are a masterpiece in the making, uniquely designed by God. Embrace your uniqueness, knowing that you have a purpose and role to fulfill in God's plan. Let go of comparison and fear and celebrate the fact that you are wonderfully different. Use your talents for God's glory, continuously seeking growth and improvement. Support and encourage others in embracing their uniqueness as well. Remember, the world needs your authentic self, so embrace who you were created to be.

Embracing your uniqueness is a lifelong journey of self-discovery, acceptance, and growth. Recognize that God created you with intention and purpose. Cultivate self-acceptance, confidence, and resilience as you navigate challenges and find your niche. Embrace diversity, collaborate with others, and inspire those around you. Your journey of embracing your uniqueness has the power to transform not only your own life but also the lives of others. Embrace who you were created to be, and let your uniqueness shine brightly in the world.

CHAPTER 3

BREAKING FREE FROM EXPECTATIONS: OVERCOMING SOCIETAL PRESSURES

LET'S begin by exploring the challenges young men face in a world that often imposes unrealistic expectations on them. You will discover how to break free from these societal pressures and find your true identity in Christ. Together, you will learn how to live authentically, embracing who you were created to be.

Section 1: The Weight of Expectations

From a young age, you are bombarded with expectations from society, family, and peers. These expectations can be overwhelming, leaving you feeling trapped and unsure of yourself . Society tells you that you need to fit into a certain mold, whether it's in your appearance, career, relationships, or achievements. But these external expectations often lead to feelings of inadequacy and the loss of your true identity.

In the Bible, you find reassurance and guidance when it comes to dealing with the weight of expectations. Psalm 139:14 reminds you that you are fearfully and wonderfully made by God. You have gifts, talents, and purposes. Your worth and identity come from being created in the image of God, not from meeting the expectations of others.

Jesus Himself faced the burden of expectations during His time on earth. The religious leaders and the crowds had certain ideas of who the Messiah should be and how He should act. However, Jesus did not conform to their expectations. He remained true to His calling and fulfilled God's plan, even if it meant disappointing those around Him.

As followers of Christ, you are called to seek God's approval above all else. Romans 12:2 encourages you not to conform to the pattern of this world but to be transformed by the renewing of your minds. You should align your thoughts and actions with God's Word and seek His guidance in making decisions.

It is important to remember that you are not alone in your struggles. Hebrews 4:15-16 tells you that Jesus can empathize with your weaknesses because He, too, faced the pressures and expectations of this world. You can approach Him with confidence, knowing that He understands and offers you grace and strength to overcome.

Finding freedom from the weight of expectations starts

with surrendering your life to God. Galatians 1:10 reminds you that you are called to live for an audience of One – God. When you seek His approval above the approval of others, you can experience true freedom and find your identity in Him.

Instead of striving to meet the expectations of the world, you should focus on discovering and embracing the unique purpose God has for us. Ephesians 2:10 reminds you that you are God's handiwork, created in Christ Jesus to do good works, which God prepared in advance for you to do. Your worth and significance come from fulfilling God's purposes, not from conforming to societal expectations.

The weight of expectations can be burdensome, but as Christians, you find solace in your identity as children of God. By seeking His approval, renewing your minds, and embracing your unique purpose, you can break free from the expectations of others. Remember that your worth and significance come from God alone, and He equips you to live according to His plans and purposes.

Section 2: Embracing Individuality

God made you different and special. You have your own talents, things you like, and ways of being. Embracing your individuality means being happy about your differences instead of trying to be like everyone else. It's about finding out who you really are and having the bravery to be yourself , even if it's not what everyone expects. Remember, you don't have to be like everyone else. Be proud of who God made you to be.

The Bible tells you in Psalm 139:14, "I praise you because I am fearfully and wonderfully made; your works are wonderful, I know that full well." This means that God made you in an amazing and special way, and you should appreciate that. In Jeremiah 1:5, God says, "Before I formed you in the womb I knew you, before you were born, I set you apart; I appointed you as a prophet to the nations." This verse shows that even before you were born, God had a plan for you.

When you embrace your individuality, you honor God's design for us. Instead of trying to fit into a mold or follow what everyone else is doing, you embrace the qualities that make you who you are. Maybe you enjoy playing music, drawing, or playing sports. Perhaps you have a knack for solving problems or making people laugh. These are the things that make you special, and they shouldn't be ignored.

In the Bible, Romans 12:6 reminds us, "Having gifts that differ according to the grace given to us, let us use them." This verse encourages you to use your unique gifts and talents to make a positive impact in the world. By embracing your individuality, you can contribute to the world in ways that no one else can.

Sometimes, it can be tempting to try to be like everyone else in order to fit in. But Proverbs 29:25 advises us, "The fear of man lays a snare, but whoever trusts in the Lord is safe." It's important to remember that your true security and happiness come from trusting in God and being true to yourself .

So, son, don't be afraid to embrace who you are. You don't have to be just like your friends or follow the crowd. God made you unique and special, and he has a purpose for your life. Embrace your individuality with confidence, knowing that you are fearfully and wonderfully made. Trust in God, use your gifts, and make a difference in the world by being the amazing person He created you to be.

Section 3: Defying Stereotypes

Society often places certain stereotypes on young men, expecting them to fit into predefined roles. You are told that you should be strong, independent, and emotionless. But the truth is, men are complex beings with a wide range of emotions and experiences. It's essential to challenge these stereotypes and embrace the fullness of your humanity. Real strength lies in vulnerability and authenticity.

The Bible provides you with examples of men who defied societal expectations and embraced their true selves. David, a shepherd boy, defied the expectations of his family and became a mighty king chosen by God. Despite facing challenges and making mistakes, he showed strength in his vulnerability as he poured out his heart to God in the Psalms.

Jesus Himself defied societal norms by displaying empathy, compassion, and a willingness to express His emotions. He wept when His friend Lazarus died and showed righteous anger when He cleansed the temple. Jesus exemplified that true strength comes from a place of love and authenticity.

As young men, you can find freedom in defying stereotypes and embracing your unique identities. You can seek God's guidance and discover who you truly are in Him. It's okay to express your emotions, to ask for help, and to be vulnerable. By doing so, you create space for genuine connections and deeper relationships with others.

We can also challenge the stereotypes society places on men by treating others with kindness, respect, and equality. You can stand against toxic masculinity and instead strive to be men of integrity, love, and compassion. By defying stereotypes, you become agents of change in a world that desperately needs authenticity and acceptance.

Remember, you are fearfully and wonderfully made in the image of God. Your emotions, your passions, and your unique qualities are part of who you are meant to be. Embrace your true self and defy the stereotypes that seek to limit you. Find strength in vulnerability, knowing that God's power is made perfect in your weaknesses. Be a beacon of authenticity, defying societal expectations and showing the world what it means to be a man created in God's image.

Section 4: Seeking God's Approval

Seeking God's approval is a powerful shift in your perspective. In the Bible, the apostle Paul reminds you in Galatians 1:10, "For am I now seeking the approval of man, or of God? Or am I trying to please man? If I were still trying to please man, I would not be a servant of Christ." This verse reminds you that your primary focus should be on pleasing God rather than seeking the approval of people.

When you seek God's approval, you align yourself with His will and purpose for your lives. You recognize that He knows you intimately and understands your true worth. Psalm 139:14 declares, "I praise you because I am fearfully and wonderfully made; your works are wonderful, I know that full well." God created you with purpose, and His approval is all you truly need.

By seeking God's approval, you are liberated from the burden of comparison. In a world obsessed with measuring up to societal standards, you can find solace in knowing that God's love for you is not based on external achievements or appearances. Romans 8:38-39 assures us, "For I am convinced that neither death nor life, neither angels nor demons, neither the present nor the future, nor any powers, neither height nor depth, nor anything else in all creation, will be able to separate us from the love of God that is in Christ Jesus your Lord." God's love is unconditional and everlasting.

When you prioritize seeking God's approval, you can

experience true freedom. You are no longer held captive by the opinions and expectations of others. Instead, you are secure in the knowledge that God accepts you just as you are. In Ephesians 1:4-5, you read, "For he chose us in him before the creation of the world to be holy and blameless in his sight. In love, he predestined us for adoption to sonship through Jesus Christ, in accordance with his pleasure and will." God has chosen you and delights in you, and His approval outweighs any fleeting validation from the world.

Seeking God's approval also shapes your priorities and actions. You strive to live in obedience to His commandments and walk in His ways. As Jesus said in John 14:15, "If you love me, keep my commands." By seeking to please God, you align your life with His will, pursuing righteousness and living a life that brings honor to His name.

Seeking God's approval is a transformative mindset. It frees you from the need for external validation and allows you to embrace your identity as beloved children of God. His love and acceptance remain constant, providing you with security and peace. Fix your eyes on pleasing God rather than seeking the approval of others, knowing that His approval is all you need to live a fulfilling and purposeful life.

Section 5: Finding Freedom in Christ

Jesus came to free you from the pressures and expectations that society puts on us. He gives you a new way to live, one that doesn't follow the world's rules but follows what God's Word says is true. When you let Jesus change you from the inside, you can break the chains that hold you back. In Jesus, you discover who you really are and the freedom to be yourself.

The Bible says in John 8:36, "So if the Son sets you free, you will be free indeed." This means that when you accept Jesus into your lives, He sets you free in a real and true way. You don't have to be controlled by what others think or what the world expects. You can find your worth and purpose in Jesus.

In Galatians 5:1, it says, "For freedom Christ has set us free; stand firm therefore, and do not submit again to a yoke of slavery." This verse reminds you that Christ has already given you freedom. You don't need to go back to the old ways of living, trying to please everyone or trying to fit in. You can stand strong and live in the freedom that Jesus offers.

When you believe in Jesus and follow Him, you can experience the freedom He offers. It's not about following the world's standards or trying to be someone we're not. It's about embracing who you are in Christ and living out the purpose God has for your lives.

Remember, God loves you just as you are, and He wants you to find freedom in Him. So, trust in Jesus, seek Him in His Word, and let Him transform you into the person He created you to be.

When you find your freedom in Christ, you discover a

deep sense of peace and joy. You no longer have to strive to meet the world's expectations or compare yourself to others. Instead, you can find contentment in knowing that you are loved and accepted by God.

The Bible tells you in 2 Corinthians 3:17, "Now the Lord is the Spirit, and where the Spirit of the Lord is, there is freedom." This means that when you have Jesus in your lives, you have true freedom. You are no longer bound by fear, doubt, or the need to impress others. Instead, you can live in the freedom of God's love and grace.

In Romans 8:1-2, it says, "Therefore, there is now no condemnation for those who are in Christ Jesus, because through Christ Jesus the law of the Spirit who gives life has set you free from the law of sin and death." This verse reminds you that in Christ, you are free from condemnation and the power of sin. You don't have to carry guilt or shame because Jesus has already paid the price for your mistakes. You can walk in the freedom of forgiveness and new life.

Finding freedom in Christ also means that you can let go of the need for worldly success and approval. Your worth is not determined by your achievements or what others think of us. Instead, your worth comes from being children of God. Ephesians 2:10 says, "For you are God's handiwork, created in Christ Jesus to do good works, which God prepared in advance for us to do." This verse reminds you that you are valuable and have a purpose in God's eyes. You can find true fulfillment by following His plans for your lives.

As young boys, it's important to remember that true freedom is found in Jesus. When you trust in Him, you can let go of the pressures of the world and live in the freedom He offers. You can be confident in who you are, knowing that you are loved, accepted, and valued by your Heavenly Father. So, let's embrace the freedom you have in Christ and live boldly for Him.

Section 6: Embracing God's Purpose for Your Life

When you find your freedom in Christ, you discover a deep sense of peace and joy. You no longer have to strive to meet the world's expectations or compare yourself to others. Instead, you can find contentment in knowing that you are loved and accepted by God.

The Bible tells you in 2 Corinthians 3:17, "Now the Lord is the Spirit, and where the Spirit of the Lord is, there is freedom." This means that when you have Jesus in your lives, you have true freedom. You are no longer bound by fear, doubt, or the need to impress others. Instead, you can live in the freedom of God's love and grace.

In Romans 8:1-2, it says, "Therefore, there is now no condemnation for those who are in Christ Jesus, because through Christ Jesus the law of the Spirit who gives life has set you free from the law of sin and death." This verse reminds you that in Christ, you are free from condemnation and the power of sin. You don't have to carry guilt or shame because

Jesus has already paid the price for your mistakes. You can walk in the freedom of forgiveness and new life.

Finding freedom in Christ also means that you can let go of the need for worldly success and approval. Your worth is not determined by your achievements or what others think of us. Instead, your worth comes from being children of God. Ephesians 2:10 says, "For you are God's handiwork, created in Christ Jesus to do good works, which God prepared in advance for us to do." This verse reminds you that you are valuable and have a purpose in God's eyes. You can find true fulfillment by following His plans for your lives.

As young boys, it's important to remember that true freedom is found in Jesus. When you trust in Him, you can let go of the pressures of the world and live in the freedom He offers. You can be confident in who you are, knowing that you are loved, accepted, and valued by your Heavenly Father. So, let's embrace the freedom you have in Christ and live boldly for Him. Embracing God's purpose for your life is a journey of trust and obedience. It requires a willingness to surrender your own desires and align your will with God's. The Bible tells you in Jeremiah 29:11, "For I know the plans I have for you," declares the Lord, "plans to prosper you and not to harm you, plans to give you hope and a future." God's plans for you are good, and He desires to lead you into a life of purpose and fulfillment.

To discover God's purpose, spend time in prayer and seek His guidance. Ask Him to reveal His will for your life and give you clarity. Trust that He will direct your steps and open doors of opportunity. Proverbs 3:5-6 reminds us, "Trust in the Lord with all your heart and lean not on your own understanding; in all your ways submit to him, and he will make your paths straight."

As you embrace God's purpose, remember that it may not always align with the world's definition of success. God's plans may lead you on a different path than you originally envisioned, but His ways are higher, and His wisdom is perfect. Trust that His purpose for your life is uniquely designed for you.

In Ephesians 2:10, you are reminded that, "we are God's handiwork, created in Christ Jesus to do good works, which God prepared in advance for us to do." You were crafted to fulfill your God-given purpose. Take time to discover and develop those gifts, using them to bring glory to God and bless others.

Embracing God's purpose also involves obedience. It may require stepping out of your comfort zone or facing challenges along the way. However, know that God will equip you and empower you to accomplish what He has called you to do. Philippians 4:13 says, "I can do all this through him who gives me strength." Rely on God's strength and trust in His provision as you walk in obedience to His purpose.

Remember, embracing God's purpose is not a one-time event, but a lifelong journey of growth and transformation. It may evolve and unfold over time as you continue to seek Him and align your life with His will. Stay connected to God through His Word, prayer, and fellowship with other believers. Surround yourself with a supportive community that encourages and challenges you to live out your purpose.

Embracing God's purpose for your life is a beautiful and fulfilling journey. Trust in His plans, seek His guidance, and surrender your own desires to Him. Develop and use your unique gifts to make a positive impact in the world. Embrace obedience and rely on God's strength as you walk in His purpose. Allow Him to lead you into a life of significance and fulfillment, knowing that He will be with you every step of the way.

Section 7: Setting Boundaries

Setting healthy boundaries is essential when breaking free from societal pressures. It involves identifying what is truly important to you and establishing limits on what you will and will not tolerate. Boundaries help protect your well-being and ensure that you prioritize your own values and beliefs. By setting boundaries, you assert control over your life and refuse to be swayed by external expectations that do not align with your true self.

In the Bible, you see examples of individuals who set boundaries to remain faithful to God's calling. Daniel, for instance, established a boundary by refusing to eat the king's food, choosing instead to follow a diet that honored God

(Daniel 1:8). Similarly, Joseph set boundaries when he resisted Potiphar's wife's advances, refusing to compromise his integrity (Genesis 39:7-12). These biblical accounts teach you the importance of setting boundaries to stay true to your faith and convictions.

As Christians, your ultimate authority for setting boundaries comes from God's Word. The Bible offers guidance on how you should live, the values you should uphold, and the behaviors you should avoid. By aligning your boundaries with biblical principles, you ensure that your choices honor God and reflect His love for us.

Setting boundaries also involves learning to say, "no" when necessary. Jesus Himself demonstrated the importance of setting boundaries when He withdrew to spend time alone in prayer (Mark 1:35). He recognized the need for rest and solitude to replenish His spirit. Likewise, you should prioritize self-care and not feel guilty for taking time to rest, recharge, and seek God's guidance.

Remember that setting boundaries is not about isolating yourself or being unkind to others. It is about maintaining healthy relationships and creating space for personal growth. Boundaries allow you to invest your time, energy, and resources in meaningful ways and avoid being overwhelmed or taken advantage of.

When setting boundaries, it's essential to communicate them respectfully and assertively. Clearly express your needs and limitations, while also being open to compromise when appropriate. By doing so, you promote healthy communication and mutual respect in your relationships.

Keep in mind that setting boundaries may not always be easy. You may face resistance or pushback from others who are accustomed to crossing your boundaries. However, remain steadfast and firm in your convictions, knowing that you are honoring God and yourself by establishing healthy limits.

Setting boundaries is crucial for breaking free from societal pressures and living according to your values and beliefs. Seek guidance from the Bible and learn from biblical examples of individuals who set boundaries to honor God. Remember to prioritize self-care, learn to say, "no" when necessary, and communicate your boundaries respectfully. As you establish healthy boundaries, you create a space for personal growth, maintain meaningful relationships, and stay true to your God-given identity. Trust in God's guidance and strength as you navigate the process of setting boundaries and find freedom and peace in embracing who you were created to be.

Section 8: Rethinking Success

Success is often portrayed in society as attaining wealth, fame, or power. However, as followers of Christ, you are called to redefine success according to God's standards. In the Bible, success is not solely measured by worldly achievements but by the alignment of your life with God's purpose.

In Joshua 1:8, God instructs Joshua, saying, "Keep this Book of the Law always on your lips; meditate on it day and night, so that you may be careful to do everything written in it. Then you will be prosperous and successful." True success comes from living according to God's Word and seeking His guidance in all that you do.

Rather than pursuing personal gain, you should prioritize living a life of integrity, love, and service. In Matthew 20:26, Jesus teaches, "Whoever wants to become great among you must be your servant." Success is found in humbly serving others, just as Jesus Himself came to serve and not to be served (Matthew 20:28).

Furthermore, success can be measured by the impact you make on the lives of others. In Acts 20:35, the apostle Paul reminds you of Jesus' words, "It is more blessed to give than to receive." True success is found in generously sharing your blessings and resources with those in need, showing compassion and extending a helping hand.

Building meaningful relationships is also a vital aspect of success. Proverbs 27:17 tells us, "As iron sharpens iron, so one person sharpens another." Success is reflected in the quality of your relationships, how you love and support one another, and how you encourage each other to grow in your faith.

Success, ultimately, is about fulfilling God's purpose for your lives. In Jeremiah 29:11, God says, "For I know the plans I have for you...plans to prosper you and not to harm you, plans to give you hope and a future." True success is aligning you with God's plans, seeking His will, and walking in obedience to His Word.

As you rethink success, focus on the eternal rather than the temporary. Strive to honor God in all areas of your lives, cultivating a heart of love, humility, and service. True success lies in living a life that pleases God and brings Him glory. May your life be a reflection of His grace and goodness, impacting others and pointing them towards the true source of success —the person of Jesus Christ.

Section 9: Embracing Emotional Well-Being

In addition to facing external challenges, your emotional well-being is also crucial to navigating life's ups and downs. The Bible recognizes the importance of your emotional health and offers guidance on how you can embrace it.

One of the key aspects of emotional well-being is self-care. Jesus Himself demonstrated the importance of rest and rejuvenation. In Mark 6:31, it says, "Then, because so many people were coming and going that they did not even have a chance to eat, he said to them, 'Come with me by yourselves to a quiet place and get some rest.'" Just as Jesus prioritized rest, you too should make time for activities that bring you joy, peace, and rejuvenation. It could be engaging in hobbies, spending time in nature, or simply taking a break from your busy schedules.

At times, you may find yourself overwhelmed by your

emotions. It's important to remember that your feelings are valid. The Bible acknowledges this in Psalm 34:18, which says, "The Lord is close to the brokenhearted and saves those who are crushed in spirit." God is aware of your emotions and cares about your well-being. You can turn to Him in prayer, pouring out your hearts and seeking His comfort and healing.

Seeking professional help is another important aspect of embracing emotional well-being. Just as you would seek medical help for physical ailments, there is no shame in seeking support for your mental health. Proverbs 15:22 reminds you of the value of seeking wise counsel, saying, "Plans fail for lack of counsel, but with many advisers, they succeed." Sometimes, professional counselors or therapists can provide the guidance and support you need to navigate through difficult emotions or challenging life circumstances.

In your journey towards emotional well-being, it's important to remember that God's grace is sufficient for us. In 2 Corinthians 12:9, God tells us, "My grace is sufficient for you, for my power is made perfect in weakness." Even in your moments of emotional vulnerability, God's grace is there to strengthen you and bring you through. You can rely on His love, comfort, and guidance as you navigate the complexities of your emotions.

Section 10: Persevering in the Face of Challenges

Embracing your uniqueness doesn't mean that challenges

won't come your way. In fact, they are often part of the journey. You may face obstacles, criticism, or setbacks along the path. During such times, remember that God's purpose for your life remains unchanged. Stay resilient and persevere, knowing that challenges can refine and strengthen you. Trust in God's guidance and keep moving forward with determination and faith.

In the Bible, you find numerous examples of individuals who faced immense challenges but persevered in their faith. Joseph, despite being sold into slavery by his own brothers and enduring years of imprisonment, ultimately rose to a position of power and saved his family from famine (Genesis 37-50). The story of David illustrates how he faced the giant Goliath with courage and reliance on God, ultimately defeating him (1 Samuel 17). The apostle Paul, despite facing persecution, imprisonment, and numerous hardships, remained steadfast in his mission to spread the gospel (2 Corinthians 11:23-28).

These stories remind you that challenges are not meant to defeat you but to build resilience and deepen your dependence on God. They teach you to trust in God's faithfulness, even when circumstances seem bleak. In James 1:2-4, you are encouraged to consider it joy when you face trials because they produce endurance and maturity in your faith. It is through challenges that your character is refined, and your faith is strengthened.

When challenges arise, it's important to seek God's

guidance and wisdom. Proverbs 3:5-6 reminds you to trust in the Lord with all your hearts and lean not on your own understanding. You can turn to God in prayer, seeking His direction and strength. He promises to give you wisdom and be with you in every trial you face (James 1:5; Isaiah 41:10).

It's also crucial to surround yourself with a supportive community of believers who can offer encouragement, prayer, and accountability. Galatians 6:2 encourages you to bear one another's burdens, sharing the load during challenging times. Seek the counsel of wise mentors and friends who can provide guidance and support.

In the face of challenges, remember that you are not alone. God is with you, and He will provide the strength and resources you need to overcome. Romans 8:37 assures you that you are more than conquerors through Christ who loves us. Keep your focus on God's promises and His unwavering love for you.

As you persevere in the face of challenges, remember that they do not define you. Your identity is rooted in Christ, and He has equipped you with everything you need to overcome. Embrace challenges as opportunities for growth, relying on God's strength and trusting in His perfect plan for your life. With God by your side, you can face any challenge with confidence, knowing that He will work all things together for your good (Romans 8:28). Keep pressing on, knowing that your perseverance will lead to a life that brings glory to God and impacts the world around you.

Wrap Up

Breaking free from societal pressures requires a conscious effort to defy expectations, embrace individuality, and seek God's approval above all else. It's about finding the strength to be true to yourself , despite the pressures to conform.

As you lean on God's wisdom and surround yourself with a supportive community, you can navigate the challenges of living authentically and discover the freedom and purpose that comes from embracing who you were created to be. Remember, you are fearfully and wonderfully made, and your true identity lies in Christ.

CHAPTER 4
SONS OF THE KING: EMBRACING YOUR SPIRITUAL IDENTITY

THIS IS SUCH A VITAL CHAPTER, and one that I know will bring excitement and power to your understanding of who you were meant to be. You are a son of the King. Your spiritual identity is not based on your own achievements or status, but on your relationship with God. Together, you will delve into the Bible to understand the depth of your identity as children of God and discover how embracing this truth can transform your lives.

Section 1: Created for Sonship

Did you know that God wants you to be part of His family? It's true! From the very beginning, God desired to have a personal relationship with His creation. He longs for you to be His son. When you accept Jesus as your Savior, you become children of God, born of His Spirit. This is not something you earn or achieve; it is a gift from God.

In the Bible, in the book of John 1:12, it says, "But to all who did receive him, who believed in his name, he gave the right to become children of God." Isn't that amazing? God offers you the incredible privilege of being part of His family. He wants to be your Father, guiding and caring for you in every aspect of your lives.

As children of God, you have a special identity and purpose. You are no longer defined by the world's standards or your past mistakes. In Romans 8:14-16, it says, "For all who are led by the Spirit of God are sons of God. For you did not receive the spirit of slavery to fall back into fear, but you have received the Spirit of adoption as sons, by whom you cry, 'Abba! Father!' The Spirit himself bears witness with your spirit that you are children of God."

Knowing that you are God's beloved children gives you confidence and security. You can approach God with boldness, knowing that He loves you unconditionally. You have direct access to Him through prayer, and He delights in hearing your hearts' desires and concerns.

Being part of God's family also means that you have an inheritance. In Ephesians 1:5-6, it says, "He predestined us for adoption to himself as sons through Jesus Christ, according to the purpose of his will, to the praise of his glorious grace, with which he has blessed us in the Beloved." God blesses you abundantly and showers you with His grace and love.

As children of God, you are called to live according to His ways. You are called to love others, show kindness, and extend forgiveness, just as your Heavenly Father has done for us. In 1 John 3:1, it says, "See what kind of love the Father has given to us, that you should be called children of God; and so you are."

Remember, as a child of God, you are deeply loved and cherished. Your identity is rooted in Him, and He has a purpose and plan for your life. Embrace your sonship in God's family and live as a reflection of His love and grace. You are created for a divine purpose, and as you walk in relationship with Him, you will experience the fullness of His blessings and the joy of being part of His eternal family.

Section 2: Inheritance of the King

In Ephesians 1:11, it says, "In Him, you have obtained an inheritance, having been predestined according to the purpose of Him who works all things according to the counsel of His will." This verse assures you that your inheritance is not based on your own merit or works, but it is a gift from God Himself.

As heirs of God, you have the privilege of calling Him your Father. Romans 8:17 tells us, "Now if you are children, then you are heirs—heirs of God and co-heirs with Christ." This means that you share in the inheritance of Jesus Christ, your Savior. Just as He has received all authority and power, you are also beneficiaries of His divine blessings.

Our inheritance goes beyond material possessions or earthly treasures. It encompasses the spiritual riches that God lavishes upon us. You have access to His grace, mercy, love, and wisdom. You are adopted into His family, embraced as His beloved children. You have the assurance of His constant presence and guidance in your lives.

Inheritance also implies a future hope. In 1 Peter 1:3-4, it says, "In His great mercy He has given you new birth into a living hope through the resurrection of Jesus Christ from the dead, and into an inheritance that can never perish, spoil or fade." Your inheritance is secure and everlasting. It extends beyond this earthly life and into eternity.

Understanding your inheritance as children of God brings confidence, joy, and a sense of purpose. It reminds you that you are not alone in your journey. You have a heavenly Father who loves you unconditionally and desires to bless you abundantly. Your inheritance empowers you to live with boldness, knowing that you are heirs of the King of kings.

Embrace your inheritance with gratitude and humility. Live in a manner that reflects your identity as children of God, walking in love, righteousness, and obedience. As you do so, you will experience the fullness of your inheritance and impact the world around you with the transformative power of God's love.

Section 3: Identity in Christ

Our identity as believers is deeply rooted in your relationship with Jesus Christ. In the Bible, you are reminded of your true identity as children of God. In Ephesians 1:5, it says, "He predestined us for adoption to sonship through Jesus Christ, in accordance with his pleasure and will." This means that God chose you to be His children, not based on your own merit or accomplishments, but out of His love and grace.

Your identity as a child of God is secure and unchanging. In Romans 8:17, it says, "Now if you are children, then you are heirs—heirs of God and co-heirs with Christ." This incredible truth reveals that you have an inheritance as God's children, sharing in the riches of His kingdom. Your worth and value are not based on your achievements, appearance, or what others think of us. Your worth is found in being loved, accepted, and chosen by God Himself.

Knowing your identity in Christ brings freedom and confidence. In 1 Peter 2:9, it says, "But you are a chosen people, a royal priesthood, a holy nation, God's special possession." You are reminded that you are chosen by God, set apart for His purposes, and part of a royal priesthood. This means that you have a significant role to play in God's kingdom.

Your identity in Christ empowers you to live with purpose and make a positive impact in the world. When you understand who you are in Him, you can live with confidence, knowing that you are loved, accepted, and equipped by God. It gives you the strength to overcome challenges and persevere in faith, knowing that your identity is firmly rooted in your relationship with Jesus.

Even when you make mistakes or fall short, your identity in Christ remains unchanged. In 2 Corinthians 5:17, it says, "Therefore, if anyone is in Christ, the new creation has come: The old has gone, the new is here!" When you surrender your life to Jesus, He transforms you into a new creation. Your past does not define you anymore. You are forgiven, redeemed, and made new.

Remember, your identity in Christ is not based on what you do, but on who you are in Him. Embrace your identity as a child of God, loved, accepted, and chosen by Him. Let this truth shape how you see yourself and how you live your life. Walk with confidence, knowing that your identity in Christ is a powerful foundation that can never be shaken. Your identity as a son of the King is not based on your own merit but on your relationship with Jesus Christ. Through Him, you are adopted into God's family, and you become His children. This identity is unchanging and secure. No matter your past mistakes or shortcomings, you are loved, accepted, and chosen by God. Your worth is not determined by what you do, but by who you are in Christ.

Section 4: Privileges and Responsibilities

Being a child of God comes with incredible privileges and responsibilities. As followers of Christ, you have the privilege of having a personal relationship with your heavenly Father. You can talk to Him anytime through prayer, knowing that He listens and deeply cares for us. In the Bible, 1 Peter 5:7 reminds you to cast all your anxieties on Him because He cares for us.

Furthermore, as children of God, you have the privilege of experiencing His abundant love, peace, and joy in your lives. In John 15:9-11, Jesus tells you that as you abide in His love and keep His commandments, His joy will remain in us. This joy goes beyond temporary happiness and is rooted in your connection with Him.

However, along with these privileges, you also have responsibilities. You are called to live in a manner that honors God and reflects His character to the world around us. In Matthew 5:16, Jesus encourages you to let your light shine before others, so that they may see your good works and give glory to your Father in heaven. Your actions, attitudes, and words should align with God's teachings, demonstrating His love, grace, and mercy to those you interact with.

As children of God, you have the responsibility to obey His commandments. In John 14:15, Jesus tells us, "If you love me, you will keep my commandments." This includes loving your neighbors, forgiving others, seeking justice, and living a life of holiness. Your obedience to God's commands is a reflection of your love for Him and your desire to follow His ways.

In addition, you have the responsibility to share the good news of Jesus Christ with others. In Matthew 28:19-20, Jesus gives the Great Commission, instructing you to go and make disciples of all nations. This means sharing the message of salvation and inviting others to experience the love and grace of God.

In summary, as children of God, you are privileged to have direct access to Him through prayer and to experience His love, peace, and joy in your lives. However, you must also take your responsibilities seriously. You are called to live in a way that honors God, obey His commandments, and reflect His character to the world. Embrace your privileges with gratitude and fulfill your responsibilities with dedication, knowing that you are called to be ambassadors of God's love and grace in a world that desperately needs Him.

Section 5: Walking in Freedom

Embracing your spiritual identity as sons of the King brings freedom. You are no longer slaves to fear, guilt, or shame. In the book of Romans, it says, "For you did not receive the spirit of slavery to fall back into fear, but you have received the Spirit of adoption as sons, by whom you cry, 'Abba! Father!'" (Romans 8:15, ESV). This means that you can approach God as your loving Father, knowing that you are accepted and loved unconditionally.

God's grace is what sets you free. Ephesians 2:8-9 reminds us, "For by grace you have been saved through faith. And this is not your own doing; it is the gift of God, not a result of works, so that no one may boast" (ESV). It is not your own efforts that earn you salvation or freedom, but it is a gift from God. You cannot earn it, but you can receive it with gratitude.

As children of God, you have the power of the Holy Spirit within you. Galatians 5:1 declares, "For freedom Christ has set us free; stand firm therefore, and do not submit again to a yoke of slavery" (ESV). The Holy Spirit empowers you to live victoriously, overcoming the challenges and temptations that come your way. He guides us, comforts us, and reminds you of the truth of God's Word.

This freedom enables you to love others as Christ loved us. Galatians 5:13 says, "For you were called to freedom, brothers. Only do not use your freedom as an opportunity for the flesh, but through love serve one another" (ESV). You are called to serve others selflessly, extending the love and grace you have received from God.

Walking in freedom also means letting go of the burdens of the past. In Philippians 3:13-14, the Apostle Paul encourages us, "But one thing I do: forgetting what lies behind and straining forward to what lies ahead, I press on toward the goal for the prize of the upward call of God in Christ Jesus" (ESV). You are not defined by your past mistakes or failures. In Christ, you have a fresh start and the freedom to pursue the purpose and calling God has for us.

As you walk in freedom, you can face challenges with confidence, knowing that God is with us. Romans 8:37 assures us, "No, in all these things you are more than conquerors through him who loved us" (ESV). You have the assurance that nothing can separate you from the love of God. You can approach each day with boldness and courage, knowing that you are walking in the freedom and victory that Christ has secured for us.

Embracing your identity as sons of the King brings freedom. You are no longer bound by fear, guilt, or shame. Through God's grace and the power of the Holy Spirit, you can live victoriously, love others, and overcome challenges. Walk in the freedom Christ has given you, leaving behind the burdens of the past and embracing the abundant life He has called you to. In Him, you are more than conquerors, and you can experience the joy and fulfillment of living as children of God.

Section 6: Growing in Relationship with the Father

To fully embrace your spiritual identity, it is essential to cultivate a deep relationship with your heavenly Father. He desires to have a personal connection with each one of us. Just as a child grows closer to their earthly father through spending time together, you can grow closer to your heavenly Father by spending time in His presence.

The Bible tells you in James 4:8, "Draw near to God, and he will draw near to you." This means that as you take intentional steps towards God, He meets you halfway. You can draw near to Him through prayer, which is simply talking to God and pouring out your hearts to Him. You can share your joys, your struggles, and your desires with Him, knowing that He cares deeply for us.

Reading the Bible is another vital way to grow in relationship with the Father. In the Scriptures, you find His words of love, encouragement, and instruction. As you meditate on His Word, you gain insight into His character and His plans for your lives. Psalm 119:105 says, "Your word is a lamp to my feet and a light to my path." The Bible illuminates the path ahead and guides you in making decisions that align with God's will.

As you spend time with your heavenly Father, you experience His love, wisdom, and guidance. You begin to understand His heart for you and His desire to see you thrive. Jesus Himself modeled this close relationship with the Father during His time on Earth. He often withdrew to lonely places to pray and seek the Father's will. By following His example, you can deepen your own connection with God.

In this relationship with the Father, you also discover your true identity. You are His beloved children, chosen and cherished by Him. Ephesians 1:5-6 reminds us, "He predestined us for adoption to himself as sons through Jesus Christ, according to the purpose of his will, to the praise of his glorious grace." When you truly grasp this truth, it transforms how you see yourself and how you approach life's challenges.

Growing in relationship with the Father is a journey that requires patience and persistence. It is about seeking Him daily, even in the midst of busyness and distractions. It is about surrendering your will to His and allowing Him to guide your steps. As you continue to seek Him, you will experience the depth of His love and the richness of His presence.

So, commit to spending time with your heavenly Father, seeking Him through prayer and reading His Word. Draw near to Him, knowing that He longs to draw near to us. As you grow in intimacy with the Father, you will discover your true identity and experience the abundant life He has prepared for us.

Section 7: United in the Family of God

As sons of the King, you are part of a larger family. You are brothers and sisters in Christ, united by your faith in Him. The body of Christ, the church, is a community where you can support, encourage, and grow together. By embracing your spiritual identity, you can foster healthy relationships within the family of God, demonstrating love, forgiveness, and unity.

In the Bible, the apostle Paul compares the church to a body, where each member has a unique role to play (1 Corinthians 12:12-27). Just as your physical bodies are made up of different parts that work together harmoniously, so too should the body of Christ function as one cohesive unit. When you understand that you are all interconnected and that each person has value and purpose, you can appreciate the importance of unity within the family of God.

Jesus Himself prayed for the unity of believers, emphasizing the impact it would have on the world. In John 17:20-23, He prayed, "I pray also for those who will believe in me through their message, that all of them may be one, Father, just as you are in me and I am in you. May they also be in us so that the world may believe that you have sent me."

Being united in the family of God means living in harmony with one another. It means putting aside differences, forgiving one another, and extending grace and love. Romans 12:16 encourages you to "live in harmony with one another" and to "associate with people of low position" without being haughty or prideful. It is in these acts of humility and kindness that you demonstrate the love of Christ and draw others into the family of God.

The family of God is not limited to your local church or denomination. It extends across geographical, cultural, and generational boundaries. Galatians 3:28 reminds you that, "There is neither Jew nor Gentile, neither slave nor free, nor is there male and female, for you are all one in Christ

Jesus." This verse highlights the inclusive nature of the family of God, where all believers are equal and united in Christ.

When you come together as the family of God, you can support one another through life's challenges, celebrate one another's victories, and grow together in your faith. Hebrews 10:24-25 encourages you to "consider how you may spur one another on toward love and good deeds, not giving up meeting together, as some are in the habit of doing, but encouraging one another." In your unity, you find strength, encouragement, and the ability to impact the world around us.

As members of the family of God, strive to build bridges instead of walls. Extend love, acceptance, and forgiveness to your fellow believers. May your unity and genuine care for one another be a testimony to the world, drawing others into the family of God. Together, live out your spiritual identity as brothers and sisters in Christ, united in love and dedicated to fulfilling God's purposes.

Section 8: Walking in Authority

As sons of the King, you are not only loved and accepted but also entrusted with authority. This authority comes from Jesus Himself, who has given you power over the forces of darkness. In the book of Luke, chapter 10, verse 19, Jesus says, "I have given you authority to trample on snakes and scorpions and to overcome all the power of the enemy; nothing will harm you."

With this authority, you have the ability to make a difference in people's lives. You can pray for others and intercede on their behalf, knowing that your prayers have the power to bring about transformation. In James 5:16, it says, "The prayer of a righteous person is powerful and effective."

When you walk in the authority given to us, you can see God's power at work in the lives of those around us. You can bring healing to the sick, deliverance to the oppressed, and restoration to the brokenhearted. In Mark 16:17-18, Jesus says, "And these signs will accompany those who believe: In my name they will drive out demons; they will speak in new tongues; they will pick up snakes with their hands; and when they drink deadly poison, it will not hurt them at all; they will place their hands on sick people, and they will get well."

It is important to remember that the authority you have comes from God, and you must exercise it with humility and obedience to His will. You should always seek His guidance and rely on the Holy Spirit to lead you in using your authority wisely.

Walking in authority also means living a life that aligns with God's Word and following His commandments. As you grow in your relationship with Him, you become more aware of the authority you possess and the responsibility that comes with it. You should strive to live a life of integrity, righteousness, and love, reflecting the character of Christ.

Walking in authority is not about exerting power over others, but about using the authority entrusted to you by Jesus to bring about positive change and advance His kingdom. Through prayer, intercession, and obedience to God's Word, you can make a real impact in the lives of those around us. Embrace your authority as children of God, knowing that He has empowered you to bring healing, deliverance, and restoration to a world in need.

Section 9: Discerning God's Voice

As children of God, you have the privilege of hearing His voice. The Bible teaches you that God speaks to His people in various ways. In John 10:27, Jesus says, "My sheep hear my voice, and I know them, and they follow me." This means that as followers of Christ, you can develop a close relationship with Him and learn to recognize His voice.

To discern God's voice, you need to cultivate a personal connection with Him. Prayer is a powerful tool that allows you to communicate with God and listen for His guidance. By setting aside dedicated time to pray and seek His presence, you create an environment where you can hear His voice more clearly.

Another important aspect of discerning God's voice is spending time in His Word, the Bible. The Scriptures are God's inspired Word, and they provide you with wisdom, guidance, and understanding. By regularly reading and studying the Bible, you become familiar with God's character and His ways. This helps you discern His voice amidst the noise and distractions of the world.

Seeking godly counsel is also beneficial in discerning God's voice. Proverbs 11:14 says, "Where there is no guidance, a people falls, but in an abundance of counselors, there is safety." When facing important decisions or seeking clarity, it can be helpful to seek counsel from mature believers who have a strong relationship with God. They can offer insight and wisdom, helping you discern God's voice more effectively.

Discerning God's voice requires patience and practice. It's important to approach the process with an open heart and a willingness to obey God's leading. Sometimes, God may speak to you through a gentle whisper, an impression, or a sense of peace. Other times, His voice may come through a confirmation in Scripture or a sermon. By staying connected to Him and seeking His voice diligently, you can discern His will and follow His leading.

It's crucial to note that discerning God's voice requires testing it against the truth of the Bible. God will never contradict His own Word. His voice will always align with His character and the principles revealed in Scripture. By comparing what you hear to the truths of the Bible, you can ensure that you are truly hearing from God.

Discerning God's voice is a precious gift available to every believer. Through prayer, studying the Bible, seeking godly counsel, and testing what you hear against

Scripture, you can grow in your ability to recognize and respond to God's voice. As you develop a close relationship with Him, you will become more attuned to His leading, enabling you to walk in alignment with His plans for your lives. May you continually seek His voice and trust in His guidance as you navigate your journey of faith.

Section 10: Impacting the World as Sons of the King

Embracing your identity as sons of the King empowers you to impact the world around us. As believers in Jesus Christ, you are adopted into God's family and become His sons and daughters (Romans 8:15-17). This identity gives you a sense of purpose, confidence, and authority to make a difference.

Just as a prince represents his father, you represent your Heavenly Father in the world. Your life become a testimony of God's love, grace, and transformational power. You have the privilege to reflect the character of your Father, who is loving, compassionate, and just.

In your everyday lives, you have countless opportunities to impact the world as sons of the King. You can bring the hope and joy of the Kingdom wherever you go. By treating others with kindness, compassion, and respect, you demonstrate the love of God. Even small acts of love, such as listening to someone in need, offering a helping hand, or speaking words of encouragement, can have a profound impact on someone's life.

Sharing the truth of the Gospel is another powerful way to impact the world. As sons of the King, you have been entrusted with the message of salvation through Jesus Christ. You can share your faith boldly, knowing that the Holy Spirit works through you to bring others into a life-changing encounter with Jesus. By sharing the Good News, you help others find their identity in Christ and experience the transformation that comes through a relationship with Him.

Our influence extends beyond personal interactions. You can impact the world through prayer, interceding for the needs of others and the advancement of God's kingdom. Prayer has the power to break chains, bring healing, and release God's purposes on earth. As sons of the King, you can pray with confidence, knowing that your prayers are heard and can bring about real change.

In all that you do, it is important to remember that your impact on the world comes from a position of humility and dependence on God. You are not trying to build your own kingdom or elevate yourself , but rather you are instruments in the hands of your Heavenly Father. It is through His strength and guidance that you can truly make a difference.

So, embrace your identity as sons of the King and step out boldly to impact the world around us. Let your life reflect the love and grace of your Heavenly Father. Share the Good News of Jesus and pray for God's kingdom to come. By doing so, you participate in bringing God's love, truth, and transformation to a world in need. As sons of the King, you have a unique role to play in advancing His kingdom on earth.

Wrap Up

Embracing your spiritual identity as sons of the King is not only a privilege but also a calling. As you recognize and live in the reality of your identity, you walk in authority, hear God's voice, impact the world, and serve with humility. Persevere in this truth, growing in your relationship with the Father, and living out your God-given purpose. May you fully embrace your identity as sons of the King and allow it to shape every aspect of your lives, bringing glory to your heavenly Father and advancing His kingdom on Earth.

CHAPTER 5
UNMASKING THE PAST: HEALING AND RESTORATION

UNMASKED the past can be tough, but it is necessary for healing from what has hurt you. You all carry wounds, hurts, and mistakes from your past, but through God's love and grace, you can find healing and restoration. Let's discover how you can let go of the past, experience God's forgiveness, and embrace a future full of hope.

Section 1: Facing the Pain

The past can be a painful place. You may have experienced broken relationships, disappointments, or even trauma. It's essential to acknowledge and face that pain instead of burying it deep within. God understands your pain and invites you to bring it to Him. Take the first step of acknowledging the hurt and seeking healing.

In the Bible, you find comfort and encouragement in God's promises. Psalm 34:18 reminds you that, "The LORD is near to the brokenhearted and saves the crushed in spirit." God is not distant from your pain; He is right there with us, ready to heal your wounds and mend your brokenness. You can pour out your hearts to Him, knowing that He cares deeply for you (1 Peter 5:7).

Facing the pain requires vulnerability and honesty. It may involve seeking professional help or confiding in a trusted friend or mentor. Proverbs 12:25 tells you that, "Anxiety in a man's heart weighs him down, but a good word makes him glad." When you share your burdens with others, you open yourself up to receive comfort, support, and wise counsel.

God also provides you with His Word as a source of healing. In Isaiah 61:1, it says, "The Spirit of the Lord GOD is upon me because the LORD has anointed me to bring good news to the poor; he has sent me to bind up the brokenhearted, to proclaim liberty to the captives, and the opening of the prison to those who are bound." God's Word has the power to bring freedom, restoration, and healing to your wounded hearts.

As you face your pain, it's important to remember that healing takes time. Just as physical wounds require time to heal, emotional and spiritual healing also require patience and trust in God's timing. Lamentations 3:22-23 reminds us, "The steadfast love of the LORD never ceases; his mercies never come to an end; they are new every morning; great is your faithfulness." God's love and mercy are ever-present, and He will guide you through the healing process.

In facing your pain, you can find strength in knowing that God can bring beauty out of ashes. He can turn your deepest wounds into testimonies of His grace and redemption. Romans 8:28 assures you that, "And you know that for those who love God all things work together for good, for those who are called according to his purpose." Even in the midst of pain, God is at work, bringing about His good purposes in your lives.

So, as you face the pain, remember that you are not alone. God is with you, ready to heal, restore, and bring beauty from the ashes. Trust in His love, seek His guidance, and allow Him to walk with you on the journey of healing. Your pain does not define you, but God's love and healing power can transform your story into one of hope and redemption.

Section 2: God's Healing Power

God's healing power is evident throughout the Bible. In Psalm 147:3, it says, "He heals the brokenhearted and binds up their wounds." This verse assures you that God is not only aware of your pain but is also ready to bring healing and wholeness to your hearts.

In the New Testament, you see Jesus as the ultimate healer. He performed miraculous healings, restoring sight to the blind, making the lame walk, and even raising the dead.

These accounts demonstrate His authority over sickness and His desire to bring healing to those who come to Him in faith.

One powerful story of healing is found in Mark 5:25-34. A woman who had been suffering from a bleeding condition for twelve years reached out in faith to touch Jesus' cloak. Immediately, she was healed, and Jesus acknowledged her faith, saying, "Daughter, your faith has healed you. Go in peace and be freed from your suffering." This story reminds you that even in your desperate situations, a simple act of faith can lead to remarkable healing.

God's healing power is not limited to physical ailments; it extends to emotional, mental, and spiritual healing as well. In Isaiah 61:1, it is written, "He has sent me to bind up the brokenhearted, to proclaim freedom for the captives and release from darkness for the prisoners." God's desire is to set you free from the burdens that weigh you down and restore you to a place of wholeness.

To experience God's healing power, you must approach Him with open hearts and a willingness to surrender your pain to Him. You can pray, pouring out your deepest hurts and seeking His healing touch. Reading and meditating on His Word can also bring comfort and hope, reminding you of His promises and faithfulness.

It's important to remember that God's healing is a process. It may not happen overnight, but as you continue to trust in Him and seek His presence, He will bring healing and restoration according to His perfect timing. Sometimes, He may choose to heal miraculously, and other times, He may use doctors, counselors, or other means as instruments of His healing touch.

During the journey of healing, it's crucial to be patient and allow God to work in your lives. Healing often involves addressing deep-seated wounds, letting go of bitterness and unforgiveness, and embracing a renewed perspective. As you walk with God through the healing process, you can find comfort in knowing that He is with you every step of the way, providing comfort, strength, and hope.

God is the ultimate healer who brings restoration to every area of your lives. You can trust in His love and power to heal your brokenness. Through faith, prayer, and surrender, you can experience His healing touch in your hearts, minds, bodies, and spirits. Lean on His promises, be patient in the process, and allow Him to bring forth His healing power in your lives.

Section 3: Receiving God's Forgiveness

Receiving God's forgiveness is a crucial step towards overcoming challenges and finding healing. In the Bible, in 1 John 1:9, it says, "If you confess your sins, he is faithful and just and will forgive us your sins and purify us from all unrighteousness." This verse reminds you that God is faithful to forgive you when you come to Him with a repentant heart.

When you carry the weight of guilt and shame, it hinders

your ability to move forward. You may feel unworthy or condemned by your past mistakes. However, God's forgiveness is a powerful antidote to those feelings. In Psalm 103:12, it says, "As far as the east is from the west, so far has he removed your transgressions from us." This verse assures you that when God forgives, He completely removes your sins from us.

To receive God's forgiveness, you must acknowledge your sins and confess them to Him. You can find comfort in the words of 1 John 1:9, knowing that God is just and faithful to forgive us. Through the sacrifice of Jesus on the cross, your sins are washed away, and you are made clean before God.

Accepting God's forgiveness requires humility and a willingness to let go of the past. It means embracing the truth that in Christ, you are made new. In 2 Corinthians 5:17, it says, "Therefore, if anyone is in Christ, the new creation has come: The old has gone, the new is here!" When you accept God's forgiveness, you can leave behind the weight of your past mistakes and step into a future filled with hope and freedom.

As you receive God's forgiveness, it's essential to also forgive yourself . Sometimes, even after you have asked for God's forgiveness, you struggle to let go of the guilt and shame. However, God's love and grace extend to every aspect of your lives, including your own self-perception. You must remember that in Christ, you are forgiven and set free from the bondage of sin.

Receiving God's forgiveness empowers you to face challenges with confidence and a renewed sense of purpose. You no longer need to be defined by your past mistakes. Instead, you can embrace the identity God has given you as His beloved children, forgiven and redeemed.

In moments of doubt or when challenges arise, you can hold on to the assurance of God's forgiveness. It serves as a reminder of His unconditional love and the freedom you have in Christ. Through His forgiveness, you can find healing, restoration, and the strength to persevere in faith.

Let us, therefore, come to God with open hearts, confessing your sins and receiving His forgiveness. May you fully embrace the truth that through Christ, you are forgiven, redeemed, and empowered to overcome any challenge that comes your way.

Section 4: Forgiving Yourself and Others

Forgiving yourself can be challenging, especially when you carry guilt and shame from past mistakes. However, God's Word reminds you that in Christ, you are forgiven and made new. In 1 John 1:9, it says, "If you confess your sins, he is faithful and just to forgive us your sins and to cleanse us from all unrighteousness." When you genuinely repent and seek God's forgiveness, He removes your sins as far as the east is from the west (Psalm 103:12).

Forgiving others can be equally difficult, especially when

they have caused you pain or harm. Yet, Jesus teaches you in Matthew 6:14-15, "For if you forgive others their trespasses, your heavenly Father will also forgive you. But if you do not forgive others their trespasses, neither will your Father forgive your trespasses." Holding onto grudges and resentment only weighs you down and hinders your own spiritual growth.

Remembering the forgiveness, you have received from God can motivate you to extend forgiveness to others. Ephesians 4:32 encourages you to "be kind to one another, tenderhearted, forgiving one another, as God in Christ forgave you." Forgiveness is an act of love and obedience to God's commandment to love your neighbors as yourself (Mark 12:31).

While forgiving others may not always result in immediate reconciliation, it sets you free from the bondage of bitterness and allows God to work in your hearts. In Romans 12:19, it says, "Beloved, never avenge yourselves, but leave it to the wrath of God, for it is written, 'Vengeance is mine, I will repay, says the Lord.'" Trusting God's justice and surrendering your hurts to Him enables you to move forward with a spirit of forgiveness and peace.

In forgiving yourself and others, you must also seek reconciliation where possible. Jesus instructs you in Matthew 5:23-24, "So if you are offering your gift at the altar and there remember that your brother has something against you, leave your gift there before the altar and go. First, be reconciled to your brother, and then come and offer your gift."

Reconciliation brings restoration and demonstrates the power of forgiveness in your relationships.

Forgiveness is a vital aspect of your Christian journey. As you receive God's forgiveness, extend that same grace and mercy to yourself and others. By forgiving, you release the burden of anger and bitterness, allowing healing and restoration to take place. Remember the words of Colossians 3:13, "Bear with each other and forgive one another if any of you has a grievance against someone. Forgive as the Lord forgave you." Through forgiveness, you can experience freedom, reconciliation, and the transformative power of God's love.

Section 5: Embracing God's Grace

Embracing God's grace is a foundational aspect of persevering through challenges. In the Bible, you find numerous examples of individuals who experienced God's grace despite their shortcomings. One such example is the Apostle Paul. Before his conversion, Paul persecuted Christians zealously. Yet, God's grace transformed him into one of the greatest advocates for Christ.

In Ephesians 2:8-9, Paul writes, "For it is by grace you have been saved, through faith—and this is not from yourselves, it is the gift of God—not by works, so that no one can boast." These verses remind you that your salvation and relationship with God are not based on your own efforts or merits. Instead, it is through God's grace that you are redeemed and made new.

When facing challenges, it is easy to fall into self-condemnation and believe that you are unworthy of God's help and provision. However, God's grace surpasses your shortcomings. He extends His love, forgiveness, and strength to you freely. You can approach Him with confidence, knowing that He embraces you with open arms.

God's grace empowers you to let go of the past and move forward in faith. In Philippians 3:13-14, Paul encourages believers to forget what is behind and strain toward what is ahead, pressing on toward the goal to win the prize for which God has called you heavenward in Christ Jesus. Embracing God's grace enables you to release the burdens of past failures and mistakes, allowing His forgiveness to wash over us.

As you embrace God's grace, you can find healing and restoration. The prophet Jeremiah reminds you of God's promise in Jeremiah 31:34: "For I will forgive their wickedness and will remember their sins no more." God's grace covers your sins and frees you from the weight of guilt and shame. You can find solace in knowing that you are accepted and loved by your Heavenly Father, no matter what you have done.

In times of challenge, you can lean on God's grace to strengthen us. In 2 Corinthians 12:9, Paul shares how God's grace sustained him during his own difficulties: "But he said to me, 'My grace is sufficient for you, for my power is made perfect in weakness.' Therefore, I will boast all the more gladly about my weaknesses, so that Christ's power may rest on me." God's grace is not only for salvation but also for every step of your journey. It empowers you to overcome challenges by relying on His strength rather than your own.

Embracing God's grace is essential for persevering through challenges. It reminds you that you are forgiven, loved, and empowered by your Heavenly Father. Let go of past mistakes and embrace the unmerited favor God offers. Allow His grace to transform your perspective, strengthen your faith, and embolden you to press on. Remember that God's grace is greater than any challenge you may face, and through His grace, you can experience victory and growth in every area of your life.

Section 6: Renewing the Mind

Healing and restoration involve renewing your minds. Your thoughts and beliefs shape your actions and emotions. The Bible tells you in Romans 12:2, "Do not conform to the pattern of this world but be transformed by the renewing of your mind." This transformation begins when you allow God's truth to penetrate your thoughts and reshape your thinking.

When you face challenges, it's easy to dwell on negative thoughts and believe lies about yourself and your circumstances. But God's Word is a powerful tool for renewing your minds. As you meditate on His promises, you can replace negative and destructive thoughts with His truth.

For example, if you're feeling overwhelmed by a difficult situation, meditate on Philippians 4:6-7, which says, "Do not be anxious about anything, but in every situation, by prayer and petition, with thanksgiving, present your requests to God. And the peace of God, which transcends all understanding, will guard your hearts and your minds in Christ Jesus."

By meditating on this verse, you shift your focus from worry to trust in God's provision and His promise of peace. As you consistently fill your mind with God's truth, your thoughts align with His perspective, and you begin to experience healing and restoration.

Another powerful verse to meditate on is Isaiah 41:10: "So do not fear, for I am with you; do not be dismayed, for I am your God. I will strengthen you and help you; I will uphold you with my righteous right hand." Whenever fear or doubt creeps in, remind yourself of God's presence, His strength, and His faithfulness.

Renewing the mind is an ongoing process. It requires discipline and intentional focus on God's Word. Surround yourself with Scripture, write down verses that speak to your situation, and repeat them aloud. Allow God's truth to become deeply rooted in your mind and heart.

As your mind is renewed, you will experience a shift in your emotions and actions. Negative thoughts will lose their grip, and you will find freedom and healing. Your renewed mind will guide you towards making choices that align with God's will and bring about restoration in your life.

Renewing the mind is a crucial part of the healing and restoration process. By replacing negative thoughts with God's truth found in His Word, you can experience transformation and find healing from the inside out. Let His truth reshapes your thinking, guide your emotions, and lead you towards a life of peace, joy, and restoration.

Section 7: Finding Support and Community

Healing is not meant to be done alone. In the Bible, you see the importance of community and the power of support in times of challenges. Proverbs 27:17 says, "As iron sharpens iron, so one person sharpens another." This verse reminds you that you need each other to grow and become stronger.

When you're facing difficulties and trying to overcome challenges, it's crucial to seek support from fellow believers. Find a community of like-minded individuals who can walk alongside you on your journey toward healing and restoration. These individuals can be friends, family members, or members of your church. They can offer a listening ear, pray for you, and provide guidance and wisdom based on their own experiences and understanding of God's Word.

In Acts 2:42-47, you read about the early believers who devoted themselves to fellowship, breaking bread, and prayer. They supported and encouraged one another, sharing their possessions and meeting each other's needs. This example highlights the power of community and the impact it can have on your lives.

In times of challenge, don't hesitate to reach out to your community. Share your struggles and ask for prayer. Lean on their support, knowing that they are there to uplift and strengthen you. Together, you can find solace, encouragement, and practical help.

Additionally, consider joining small groups or Bible studies within your church. These groups provide a more intimate setting where you can build deeper relationships, share your struggles, and receive prayer and support. It's a place where you can grow spiritually and find encouragement from others who are on a similar journey.

Remember, God has designed you to thrive in community. Ecclesiastes 4:9-10 says, "Two are better than one because they have a good return for their labor: If either of them falls down, one can help the other up." you were never meant to face challenges alone. By seeking support and finding a community, you open yourself up to the love, care, and encouragement that God provides through His people.

Finding support and community is vital when facing challenges. Surround yourself with fellow believers who can walk alongside you, offer support, and pray for you. Lean on the wisdom and encouragement of those who have gone through similar experiences. Remember that you are stronger together and that God works through community to bring healing and restoration. Seek out support, build relationships, and experience the power of God's love through the community of believers.

Section 8: Moving Forward with Hope

As you unmask the past and experience healing, remember that God has a future full of hope for you. In the Bible, Jeremiah 29:11 says, "For I know the plans I have for you," declares the Lord, "plans to prosper you and not to harm you, plans to give you hope and a future." This verse reminds you that God has a specific plan and purpose for your lives, and it is a plan filled with hope.

No matter what challenges you have faced in the past, God's love and grace are greater. He offers forgiveness, redemption, and a fresh start. As you move forward, trust in

His guidance and lean on His promises. Allow His love to heal your wounds and restore your spirit.

In this new chapter of your life, keep your focus on God. Seek His wisdom, direction, and strength. Psalm 119:105 says, "Your word is a lamp for my feet, a light on my path." The Bible serves as a guide, providing wisdom and guidance for every step you take.

Remember that moving forward with hope doesn't mean the absence of difficulties. Challenges may still arise, but with God by your side, you can face them with courage and confidence. Romans 8:28 assures you that "we know that in all things God works for the good of those who love him, who have been called according to his purpose." Even in the midst of trials, God can use them for your growth and His glory.

As you embark on this new journey, surround yourself with a supportive Christian community. Hebrews 10:24-25 encourages you to "consider how you may spur one another on toward love and good deeds, not giving up meeting together, as some are in the habit of doing, but encouraging one another." Together, you can uplift and encourage each other, reminding one another of God's faithfulness and the hope you have in Him.

Finally, embrace this new chapter of your life with gratitude and a heart of surrender. Thank God for His faithfulness in the past and trust Him with your future. Proverbs 3:5-6 reminds us, "Trust in the LORD with all your heart and lean not on your own understanding; in all your ways submit to him, and he will make your paths straight."

Moving forward with hope means placing your trust in God, following His leading, and surrendering your plans and desires to Him. With Him as your guide, you can step into the future with confidence, knowing that He has good things in store for you. Keep your eyes fixed on Him, and let His hope propel you forward into the abundant life He has prepared for you.

Section 9: Learning from the Past

While the past can be painful, it is also a valuable teacher. In the Bible, you find numerous examples of individuals who faced challenges and learned important lessons along the way. One such example is the story of Joseph.

Joseph, despite facing betrayal by his own brothers, ended up in Egypt as a slave. He could have allowed bitterness and resentment to consume him, but instead, he chose to trust in God and learn from his experiences. Through God's guidance and Joseph's unwavering faith, he rose from being a prisoner to becoming a prominent leader in Egypt.

Looking back on his past, Joseph recognized that God had a greater purpose for his life. He said to his brothers, "You intended to harm me, but God intended it for good to accomplish what is now being done, the saving of many lives" (Genesis 50:20, NIV). Joseph understood that his past struggles and hardships were ultimately part of God's plan for him.

In your own lives, you can learn from Joseph's example. When you face difficulties, you must remember that God can bring good out of even the most challenging situations. Reflecting on your past experiences allows you to identify patterns or behaviors that may have contributed to pain or mistakes. By learning from the past, you can make wiser choices in the future and avoid repeating the same errors.

The Apostle Paul also provides insight into learning from the past. In his letter to the Philippians, he writes, "Brothers and sisters, I do not consider myself yet to have taken hold of it. But one thing I do: Forgetting what is behind and straining toward what is ahead, I press on toward the goal to win the prize for which God has called me heavenward in Christ Jesus" (Philippians 3:13-14, NIV).

Paul understood the importance of letting go of past failures and focusing on what lies ahead. He recognized that dwelling on past mistakes can hinder your progress in fulfilling God's purpose for your lives. Instead, he urged you to press on and strive towards the goal God has set before us.

Learning from the past does not mean dwelling on regrets or dwelling in guilt. Rather, it means seeking wisdom and discernment from God as you reflect on your experiences. You can ask God to reveal any areas where you need to grow and change. Through prayer and studying God's Word, you gain insight and direction for the future.

So, as you reflect on your past, remember that God can use your experiences, both positive and negative, to shape you into the person He has created you to be. Learn from the lessons of the past, seek God's guidance, and press on toward the purpose and goals that He has for your life. Trust that God can bring beauty out of ashes and turn your past into a steppingstone towards growth and transformation.

Section 10: Cultivating Self-Compassion

In the process of healing and restoration, it is essential to cultivate self-compassion. Often, you can be your harshest critics, replaying past mistakes and dwelling on your shortcomings. Instead, practice self-compassion by treating yourself with kindness, understanding, and forgiveness. Just as God extends His grace and mercy to you, extend the same grace and mercy to yourself. Embrace your worth as a beloved child of God, and let self-compassion guide you towards healing.

Remember the words of Psalm 103:8-13, which say, "The Lord is compassionate and gracious, slow to anger, abounding in love... As a father has compassion on his children, so the Lord has compassion on those who fear him." God's compassion knows no bounds, and He desires for you to experience that same compassion towards yourself.

When you make mistakes or face challenges, remember that God's love for you remains constant. Romans 8:1 reminds you that "there is now no condemnation for those who are in Christ Jesus." Allow this truth to sink deep into your heart. God's forgiveness is available to you, and He wants you to extend that forgiveness to yourself as well.

In Matthew 22:39, Jesus teaches you to "love your neighbor as yourself." Notice that He assumes you already love yourself . It is not selfish to show yourself compassion and love. In fact, it is an important part of living out the commandment to love others.

Be gentle with yourself. When you fall short, acknowledge your mistakes, but don't beat yourself up over them. Remember that you are a work in progress, and God is patient with you. Embrace the opportunity for growth and learning from your experiences.

Prayer can be a powerful tool in cultivating self-compassion. Take time to pray and ask God to help you see yourself through His eyes. Ask Him to help you embrace His grace and extend it to yourself. Let His love fill you and heal any wounds of self-condemnation or self-doubt.

In cultivating self-compassion, you will find greater freedom to embrace God's plan for your life. You will be able to move forward with confidence, knowing that you are loved and accepted by the Creator of the universe. As you extend compassion to yourself, you will also be able to extend it to others, creating a ripple effect of love and healing in the world.

Remember, you are fearfully and wonderfully made in the

image of God. Embrace your worth and value, and let self-compassion guide you on the journey of healing and restoration.

Wrap Up

Unmasking the past and experiencing healing and restoration is a journey that requires courage, vulnerability, and a reliance on God's love and grace. Face the pain, receive God's forgiveness, and extend forgiveness to yourself and others. Embrace God's grace and renew your mind with His truth.

Seek support and community as you navigate the healing process. With hope as your guide, step into the future that God has prepared for you. Remember, you are not defined by your past but by the work of healing and restoration that God is doing in your life.

CHAPTER 6
CHASING PURPOSE: DISCOVERING GOD'S CALL FOR YOUR LIFE

DO you know that God has a unique plan for your life? I want to walk you through the process of discovering God's call and purpose for your life. You have a unique role to play in God's grand plan. By aligning your life with His purpose, you can find fulfillment, joy, and make a positive impact in the world around us.

Section 1: Seeking God's Will

Seeking God's will is a journey that requires patience and trust. As you pray and seek His guidance, remember the words of Proverbs 3:5-6, which say, "Trust in the LORD with all your heart and lean not on your own understanding; in all your ways submit to him, and he will make your paths straight."

Another important aspect of seeking God's will is immersing yourself in His Word, the Bible. The Bible is like a roadmap that provides guidance and wisdom for every aspect of life. Psalm 119:105 reminds you that, "Your word is a lamp for my feet, a light on my path." As you study and meditate on God's Word, you will gain insight into His character and His desires for your life.

It's also beneficial to seek counsel from mature Christians who can provide godly wisdom and guidance. Proverbs 15:22 says, "Plans fail for lack of counsel, but with many advisers, they succeed." Surround yourself with believers who can offer biblical perspectives and help you discern God's will.

As you seek God's will, be open to His leading and willing to surrender your own desires. Jesus taught you in Matthew 16:24, "Whoever wants to be my disciple must deny themselves and take up their cross and follow me." Surrendering to God means putting His plans above your own and trusting that His ways are higher and better than your own.

Remember, seeking God's will is not a one-time event but an ongoing process. It requires a daily commitment to aligning your heart and desires with His. Be patient and trust that God will reveal His plan in His perfect timing. Proverbs 3:6 assures us, "In all your ways submit to him, and he will make your paths straight."

Seeking God's will is an essential part of understanding your purpose and fulfilling His plan for your life. Through prayer, studying His Word, seeking counsel, and surrendering your own desires, you can navigate the journey of discovering God's will. Trust that He is faithful, and as you seek Him wholeheartedly, He will guide you and make your path clear. May you embark on this journey with faith and anticipation, knowing that God's plan for your life is far greater than anything you could imagine.

Section 2: Listening to God's Voice

Listening to God's voice is essential when facing challenges. In the Bible, you see how God spoke to His people and provided guidance in difficult times. One example is found in Proverbs 3:5-6, which says, "Trust in the LORD with all your heart, and do not lean on your own understanding. In all your ways acknowledge him, and he will make straight your paths." These verses remind you to trust in God and seek His direction.

To listen to God's voice, you must create space for quiet reflection and prayer. Just as Jesus often withdrew to a solitary place to pray (Luke 5:16), you can find solace in seeking God's presence. As you quiet your minds and hearts, you become more receptive to His voice.

Additionally, seeking wise counsel from fellow believers can help you discern God's voice. Proverbs 11:14 tells us, "Where there is no guidance, a people fall, but in an abundance of counselors there is safety." God may speak to you through the wise advice and insights of others who are grounded in His Word.

Sometimes, God's guidance comes through the alignment of circumstances. Doors may open or close, opportunities may arise, or a deep sense of peace may accompany a decision. God can use these external factors to guide your steps, as you trust in Him and surrender your plans to His greater purpose.

It's important to remember that listening to God's voice requires patience and practice. Just as you develop any relationship through regular communication, your relationship with God grows as you intentionally seek His voice. The more you align your hearts with His, the clearer His guidance becomes.

In times of challenges, it can be tempting to rely solely on your own understanding or seek quick solutions. However, when you take the time to listen to God's voice, you tap into His wisdom and guidance. He knows the best path for you and desires to lead you toward His purposes.

As you face challenges, take intentional steps to listen to God's voice. Spend time in His Word, seek wise counsel, and create moments of quiet reflection. Trust that as you tune in to His voice, He will guide your steps and provide the wisdom and strength you need to overcome any obstacle. Remember the promise found in Isaiah 30:21, "And your ears shall hear a word behind you, saying, 'This is the way, walk in it,' when you turn to the right or when you turn to the left."

Section 3: Discovering Your Passions and Gifts

God has created you with unique passions, talents, and gifts. These are not random, but intentionally given by Him. The Bible tells you in Psalm 139:14 that you are fearfully and wonderfully made. God has woven specific qualities into your being for a purpose.

Take the time to explore what brings you joy and fulfillment. What activities make your heart come alive? What do you find yourself naturally drawn to? These can be indications of your God-given passions.

Additionally, consider the talents and skills that you possess. Are you good at playing an instrument, writing, problem-solving, or working with your hands? These abilities are gifts from God, and He wants you to use them for His glory.

In Romans 12:6, the apostle Paul reminds you that you have different gifts according to the grace given to us. God has given you these gifts to serve others and build up His kingdom.

As you seek to understand your passions and gifts, spend time in prayer and reflection. Ask God to reveal His purpose for your life and to guide you in discovering how you can use your unique qualities to make a difference in the world.

Look to the examples in the Bible for inspiration. Moses doubted his ability to speak, but God equipped him to lead the Israelites out of Egypt (Exodus 4:10-12). David used his musical talent to worship and praise God (1 Samuel 16:23). The apostle Paul used his intellect and zeal to spread the Gospel (Acts 9:15-16).

Remember that discovering your passions and gifts is an ongoing process. It may take time and exploration to fully understand how God wants to use you. Be open to new experiences and opportunities that allow you to use your gifts.

Seek the guidance of wise and mature believers who can provide insights and encouragement along the way. They can help you discern your passions and offer guidance as you navigate your path.

Ultimately, the goal is to use your passions and gifts to bring glory to God and to serve others. As you align your life with God's purpose, you will find fulfillment and joy in living out the unique plan He has for you.

So, take time to discover your passions, embrace your gifts, and trust that God will lead you to fulfill the purpose He has for your life. You are a unique creation, designed by God for a specific reason. Embrace who you are and seek to make a difference in the world through the talents and passions He has given you.

Section 4: Seeking Confirmation

In your journey of understanding your God-given mission, it can be beneficial to seek confirmation from those who know you well and have a strong relationship with God.

These individuals can offer valuable insights and guidance as you navigate your desires and dreams. Just as the Bible says in Proverbs 15:22, "Without counsel plans fail, but with many advisers, they succeed."

When considering the path, you want to pursue, it is wise to share your aspirations with trusted mentors, friends, or family members who have a deep understanding of your character and a strong connection with God. They can provide valuable perspectives and help you discern if your desires align with God's will for your lives.

By seeking counsel from mature believers, you open yourself up to their wisdom and experience. They can offer guidance based on their own journey with God and help you see things from different angles. Proverbs 20:18 reminds us, "Plans are established by seeking advice; so, if you wage war, obtain guidance."

Trusted mentors or spiritual leaders can also pray with you and for us, seeking God's guidance and confirmation. The apostle Paul, in his letter to the Colossians, wrote, "We continually ask God to fill you with the knowledge of his will through all the wisdom and understanding that the Spirit gives" (Colossians 1:9).

However, it is important to note that seeking confirmation from others should not replace your personal relationship with God. Ultimately, God is the one who knows you best and has a perfect plan for your lives. Through prayer, studying His

Word, and seeking His presence, you can find assurance and clarity.

As you seek confirmation from trusted individuals, remain open to their counsel and evaluate it alongside God's Word. If their advice aligns with biblical principles and resonates with your own understanding of God's leading, it can serve as an affirmation of the path you are considering.

Remember, seeking confirmation is not about seeking validation for your desires but about aligning your will with God's will. Proverbs 16:3 encourages you to commit your plans to the Lord, saying, "Commit to the Lord whatever you do, and he will establish your plans."

Confirmation from trusted mentors, friends, or family members who walk with God can provide valuable guidance and insights as you discern your God-given mission. Their wisdom and prayers can help confirm whether your desires align with God's will. However, you must always evaluate their counsel alongside the truth of God's Word and maintain a personal relationship with Him. Seek God's guidance, commit your plans to Him, and trust that He will establish your paths.

Section 5: Embracing God's Timing

Finding your purpose is like going on an adventure that needs you to be patient and trust in God's timing. You might feel excited and want to discover and fulfill your purpose immediately. But remember, God's timing is always just right. He knows what is best for you and plans everything for your benefit. Believe that He will reveal His plan at the perfect time. During this waiting period, focus on strengthening your bond with Him and getting ready for the special task He has for you.

The Bible says in Ecclesiastes 3:1, "For everything there is a season, and a time for every matter under heaven." This means that every event in your life has a proper time and purpose, and God is the one who decides when it will happen.

In Psalm 27:14, it says, "Wait for the Lord; be strong, and let your heart take courage; wait for the Lord!" This verse encourages you to be patient, remain strong, and have courage while waiting for God's timing. It reminds you that God's plan is worth waiting for, and He will give you the strength to endure the waiting period.

Another verse that brings comfort is Isaiah 40:31, which says, "But they who wait for the Lord shall renew their strength; they shall mount up with wings like eagles; they shall run and not be weary; they shall walk and not faint." This verse assures you that those who patiently wait for the Lord will be rewarded. God will renew their strength and empower them to accomplish great things.

Remember, God's timing is perfect. He has a wonderful plan for your life. Trust in Him, grow in your relationship with Him, and be ready for the amazing purpose He has in store for you.

It's important to understand that God's timing is different from your own. While you may desire instant results, God sees the bigger picture and knows the right time for everything to fall into place. Just like a skilled conductor directs a beautiful symphony, God orchestrates the events in your life for your ultimate good.

In the Bible, you find the story of Joseph, who experienced many hardships and setbacks before his purpose was fulfilled. Despite being sold into slavery and imprisoned, Joseph remained faithful and trusted in God's timing. Eventually, God elevated him to a position of great authority, where he was able to save his family and many others from a severe famine (Genesis 37-50).

Similarly, David, who would later become the king of Israel, had to endure a long period of waiting before his purpose was realized. After being anointed as king by the prophet Samuel, David spent years fleeing from King Saul, who sought to kill him. However, through it all, David maintained his trust in God's timing and his faith in God's promises (1 Samuel 16-31).

These stories teach you valuable lessons about embracing God's timing. They remind you that even during periods of waiting and uncertainty, you should remain steadfast in your faith and continue to seek God. As you grow in your relationship with Him, you develop the strength, wisdom, and character necessary to fulfill your purpose.

In Romans 8:28, the apostle Paul writes, "And you know

that for those who love God all things work together for good, for those who are called according to his purpose." This verse assures you that God works everything out for your benefit and according to His purpose. Even if you don't understand the reasons behind your waiting, you can trust that God is working behind the scenes, preparing you for something extraordinary.

So, my young friend, be encouraged and patient as you wait for God's timing to unfold. Use this time to grow closer to Him, studying His Word, praying, and seeking His guidance. Trust that He has a unique purpose for your life, and when the time is right, He will reveal it to you. In the meantime, hold on to His promises, knowing that He is faithful and will guide you every step of the way.

Section 6: Taking Steps of Faith

Once you have a sense of God's call and purpose for your life, it's time to take steps of faith. The Bible teaches you about the power of faith and how it can move mountains. In Hebrews 11:1, it says, "Now faith is confidence in what you hope for and assurance about what you do not see." This means that even though you may not see the full picture or know how things will work out, you can have confidence and trust in God's plan.

Taking steps of faith often requires you to step out of your comfort zones. It may mean doing something that feels uncomfortable or unfamiliar. In Joshua 1:9, God encourages Joshua, saying, "Be strong and courageous. Do not be afraid; do not be discouraged, for the Lord your God will be with you wherever you go." God is with you in your moments of fear and uncertainty, giving you the strength to overcome.

Sometimes, taking steps of faith means making sacrifices. It may involve giving up something you hold dear or letting go of your own plans and desires. In Luke 9:23, Jesus tells His disciples, "Whoever wants to be my disciple must deny themselves and take up their cross daily and follow me." Following Jesus requires you to surrender your own will and trust in His perfect will for your lives.

When you take steps of faith, you can be confident that God will provide everything you need. In Philippians 4:19, it says, "And my God will meet all your needs according to the riches of his glory in Christ Jesus." God is your provider, and He knows exactly what you need to fulfill His purpose for us.

Remember, taking steps of faith is not always easy, but it is worth it. It's a journey of trust, reliance, and obedience to God. Each step you take brings you closer to fulfilling your God-given mission and experiencing the fullness of His blessings.

As you embark on your journey of faith, pray for guidance and wisdom. Seek God's direction in His Word and listen to the promptings of the Holy Spirit. Surround yourself with a supportive Christian community that can encourage and uplift you along the way.

So, take that first step today. Trust in God's plan, have courage, and rely on His strength. Step out of your comfort zone, make sacrifices, and watch as God works miracles in and through your life. Remember, faith is not about having all the answers or knowing the outcome; it's about trusting in the One who holds your future in His hands.

Section 7: Impacting the World

Discovering your purpose is not just about personal fulfillment; it's also about making a positive impact in the world. Your purpose is connected to God's greater plan of redemption and reconciliation. In the Bible, you are reminded of your call to be the salt and light of the world (Matthew 5:13-16). You are called to bring flavor and illumination to a world in need.

Jesus set the ultimate example of impacting the world through His ministry on Earth. He healed the sick, comforted the brokenhearted, and preached the good news of the kingdom. He calls you to follow in His footsteps and continue His work.

In Acts 1:8, Jesus tells His disciples, "But you will receive power when the Holy Spirit comes on you; and you will be my witnesses in Jerusalem, and in all Judea and Samaria, and to the ends of the earth." This verse emphasizes the global nature of your mission. You are called to impact not only your immediate surroundings but also the wider world.

As you align your life with God's purpose, seek opportunities to serve others, share the love of Christ, and make a difference in your community and beyond. Every act of kindness, every word of encouragement, and every expression of love has the potential to impact someone's life and bring them closer to God.

Remember the parable of the Good Samaritan (Luke

10:25-37), where a man showed compassion and care to a stranger in need. Through his actions, he demonstrated the true meaning of loving your neighbors as yourself . Likewise, by extending a helping hand, showing compassion, and being a source of hope, you can impact the world around you.

It's not just about big gestures or grand missions. Sometimes, the most profound impact comes from simple acts of kindness and faithfulness in your everyday lives. It can be as simple as listening to a friend in need, praying for someone who is hurting, or offering a helping hand to those less fortunate.

Take the time to pray and seek God's guidance on how He wants you to impact the world. He has given you unique gifts, talents, and opportunities to be His hands and feet. Embrace your role as a vessel of His love and grace, and trust that He will use you to bring about transformation in the lives of others.

Impacting the world is not a distant dream or reserved for a select few. It is a calling for every believer. Your purpose is intricately connected to God's plan of redemption. Seek opportunities to serve, love, and share the good news of Christ. Remember, even the smallest acts of kindness can have an eternal impact. Step out in faith, trust in God's leading, and watch as He uses you to make a positive difference in the world.

Section 8: Overcoming Challenges

Overcoming challenges is a recurring theme throughout the Bible. In the Old Testament, you see how Joseph faced numerous challenges, from being sold into slavery by his brothers to being wrongly accused and imprisoned. But through it all, Joseph remained faithful to God and eventually became a great leader in Egypt, saving many lives.

In the New Testament, the apostle Paul faced countless challenges as he spread the message of Christ. He endured persecution, imprisonment, and even shipwrecks. Yet, Paul remained steadfast in his faith and wrote encouraging letters to the early Christian communities, reminding them to persevere in the face of challenges.

One verse that offers comfort and guidance during challenging times is found in James 1:2-4: "Consider it pure joy, my brothers and sisters, whenever you face trials of many kinds because you know that the testing of your faith produces perseverance. Let perseverance finish its work so that you may be mature and complete, not lacking anything."

This verse reminds you that challenges can be opportunities for growth and that God can use them to develop perseverance and maturity within us. It encourages you to approach challenges with a positive mindset, knowing that they have the potential to strengthen your faith and shape you into the people God intends you to be.

Another encouraging passage is found in Philippians 4:13: "I can do all things through Christ who strengthens me." This verse reminds you that you don't have to face challenges in your own strength. With Christ by your side, you have the power to overcome any obstacle that comes your way. It's a reminder that your strength comes from Him, and He is always with us, guiding and empowering you to face and conquer challenges.

When challenges arise, it's important to turn to God in prayer. Seek His guidance, wisdom, and strength. The Bible assures you in Jeremiah 33:3, "Call to me and I will answer you and tell you great and unsearchable things you do not know." God is always ready to hear your prayers and provide you with the wisdom and direction you need to overcome challenges.

Lastly, it's essential to surround yourself with a supportive Christian community. Share your challenges with fellow believers who can offer encouragement, support, and prayer. Together, you can uplift one another and remind each other of God's faithfulness in the midst of difficulties.

Remember, challenges are not meant to discourage or defeat you. They are opportunities for growth, learning, and drawing closer to God. Trust in His promises, lean on His strength, and persevere with unwavering faith. As you overcome challenges, you will become a testimony to God's faithfulness and discover the depth of your own resilience.

Section 9: Embracing Flexibility

In your journey of understanding God's plan for your

lives, it's crucial to embrace flexibility. While having a clear sense of purpose is important, you must also be open to God's leading and remain adaptable. The Bible reminds you in Proverbs 16:9, "In their hearts humans plan their course, but the LORD establishes their steps."

God's plans for you may not always align with your own expectations or desires. He may present new opportunities or redirect your path in ways you never imagined. It's important to stay attuned to His voice and be willing to adjust your plans accordingly. As the apostle James wrote in James 4:13-15, "Now listen, you who say, 'Today or tomorrow you will go to this or that city, spend a year there, carry on business and make money.' Instead, you ought to say, 'If it is the Lord's will, you will live and do this or that.'"

Remaining flexible requires humility and trust in God's wisdom. You must surrender your own agenda and be willing to follow His guidance, even if it leads you in unexpected directions. This flexibility allows you to fully embrace God's plan for your life and experience His abundant blessings.

In the book of Jeremiah, you see an example of flexibility in the prophet's life. God called Jeremiah to be a prophet to the nations, but the specific details of his assignment were revealed progressively. Jeremiah had to remain flexible and obedient as God unfolded His plan step by step.

As you navigate through life, you can take inspiration from Jeremiah and other biblical figures who embraced flexibility. Their stories teach you the importance of trusting

God's leading and being open to His divine interruptions. When you are flexible, you position yourself to experience the fullness of God's purposes and blessings.

Flexibility doesn't mean compromising your values or principles. It means aligning your hearts with God's will and being willing to adjust your plans according to His guidance. It's about embracing the unexpected with faith and understanding that God's ways are higher than ours.

So, as you seek to understand God's plan for your life, remember to hold your plans with an open hand. Trust in His wisdom and timing. Stay flexible and adaptable, ready to follow wherever He leads. As Proverbs 3:5-6 advises, "Trust in the LORD with all your heart and lean not on your own understanding; in all your ways submit to him, and he will make your paths straight."

Embracing flexibility allows you to fully embrace the adventure of following God's plan, knowing that He is leading you to a purposeful and fulfilling life. Stay open, stay humble, and stay flexible as you journey with Him.

Section 10: Encouraging Others On Their Journey

As you continue on your own purpose journey, don't forget to encourage, and support others who are seeking to discover and pursue their purpose. The Bible reminds you in 1 Thessalonians 5:11, "Therefore encourage one another and build one another up, just as you are doing."

Share your own experiences, insights, and lessons learned with those around you. Let them know that they are not alone in their search for purpose. Offer a listening ear, providing a safe space for them to express their doubts, fears, and aspirations. Be patient and understanding, recognizing that everyone's journey is unique and unfolds at its own pace.

Be a source of inspiration by living out your purpose with authenticity and passion. Let your actions speak louder than words, showing others what it looks like to pursue God's calling in your own life. Allow your experiences and successes to serve as a beacon of hope for those who may be feeling lost or discouraged.

Offer guidance and practical advice to those who may be struggling to identify their purpose. Point them to God's Word, which is filled with wisdom and guidance. Share relevant Bible verses that speak to the topic of purpose and encourage them to seek God's guidance through prayer and meditation.

Above all, be an encourager. Speak words of affirmation and positivity into the lives of others. Remind them of their inherent worth and value in God's eyes. Help them see their potential and the unique gifts and talents they possess. Let them know that they are capable of making a difference in the world.

Remember that encouraging others on their purpose journey is not a one-time effort. It is an ongoing commitment to be there for others in their times of need. Be willing to walk alongside them, providing support and encouragement through the ups and downs of their journey.

Together, as a community of purpose-seekers, you can uplift and empower one another to live out God's call for your lives. Hebrews 10:24-25 reminds us, "And let us consider how to stir up one another to love and good works, not neglecting to meet together, as is the habit of some, but encouraging one another, and all the more as you see the Day drawing near."

By encouraging others on their purpose journey, you create a ripple effect of positivity and empowerment. Your words and actions can ignite a spark of hope and motivation in their hearts, propelling them forward in their pursuit of God's plan. Together, you can support each other in making a lasting impact on the world around you, fulfilling the purpose for which you were created.

Wrap Up

Discovering God's call and purpose for your life is an exciting and fulfilling journey. Seek His will through prayer, Scripture, and listening to His voice. Pay attention to your passions and gifts, seeking confirmation from trusted mentors. Embrace God's timing and take steps of faith as you pursue your purpose. Remember, your purpose is not just for personal fulfillment but to impact the world for God's glory. Trust that as you chase after your purpose, God will guide and empower you every step of the way.

CHAPTER 7
BATTLING INSECURITY: STRENGTHENING YOUR IDENTITY IN CHRIST

IT'S easy to get lost on the complexities of who you are and who did God create you to be. That's the simple part. God created you to be you. Still, many struggle with the boldness to be that unique and amazing creation because of insecurity. You will explore how you can strengthen your identity in Christ and overcome the doubts and insecurities that may hinder you from living the abundant life God has intended for you.

Section 1: The Battle with Insecurity

Insecurity can be a powerful and overwhelming emotion. It often stems from comparing yourself to others or feeling inadequate in certain areas of your lives. You may look at the achievements, talents, or appearances of others and feel like you fall short. It's easy to get caught up in the trap of insecurity, constantly questioning your worth and value.

However, as followers of Christ, you must remember that your true identity is found in Him. The Bible tells you that you are fearfully and wonderfully made (Psalm 139:14) and that you are created in the image of God (Genesis 1:27). Your worth and value are not determined by your accomplishments or what others think of us, but by the fact that you are beloved children of God.

When you feel insecure, you can turn to the truth of God's Word. It reminds you that you are deeply loved by your Heavenly Father (John 3:16) and that He has a unique purpose for your life (Jeremiah 29:11). You can find comfort in knowing that God accepts you just as you are and that His grace is more than sufficient for you (2 Corinthians 12:9).

Instead of comparing yourself to others, you can focus on developing your God-given gifts and talents. The Apostle Paul reminds you in Romans 12:6 that you each have different gifts according to the grace given to us. By embracing and using your unique abilities for God's glory, you can find fulfillment and confidence in who He has created you to be.

Overcoming insecurity requires renewing your minds with the truth of God's Word. You must reject the lies and negative thoughts that fuel your insecurity and replace them with the truth of who you are in Christ. Memorizing and meditating on Scripture that affirms your identity in Him can help to combat insecurity and build your confidence.

Additionally, seeking support and encouragement from fellow believers can make a significant difference. Surrounding yourself with a community of faith that uplifts, supports, and reminds you of your identity in Christ can help you overcome insecurity. Together, you can encourage one another and remind each other of the truth found in God's Word.

Insecurity is a battle that many of you face, but you don't have to fight it alone. By turning to God, immersing yourself in His Word, and leaning on the support of your Christian community, you can confront and overcome insecurity. As you grow in your understanding of your identity in Christ, you can find freedom, confidence, and a deep sense of security in Him.

Section 2: Embracing God's Truth

One of the most effective ways to combat insecurity is by filling your minds with God's truth. The Bible is a powerful resource that contains promises and affirmations of who you are in Christ. When you immerse yourself in His Word, it reminds you of your worth and value in God's eyes. Let's explore some Bible verses that can help you embrace God's truth and diminish the power of insecurity in your lives.

1. Psalm 139:14 (NIV) - "I praise you because I am fearfully and wonderfully made; your works are wonderful; I know that full well."

This verse reminds you that you are fearfully and wonderfully made by God Himself. You are His masterpiece, intricately designed with purpose and value. When you internalize this truth, it diminishes the insecurities that try to overshadow your sense of worth.

2. 1 Peter 2:9 (NIV) - "But you are a chosen people, a royal priesthood, a holy nation, God's special possession, that you may declare the praises of him who called you out of darkness into his wonderful light."

God has chosen us to be His people, a treasured possession. You have been called out of darkness and into His marvelous light. This truth reminds you that you have a significant role to play in God's kingdom and that you are deeply loved and valued by Him.

3. Ephesians 2:10 (NIV) - "For you are God's handiwork, created in Christ Jesus to do good works, which God prepared in advance for us to do."

We are God's handiwork, created with a purpose. He has prepared good works for you to do, and He equips you to fulfill them. This truth assures you that you have unique gifts and abilities that are valuable in fulfilling God's plans for your lives.

4. Romans 8:37-39 (NIV) - "No, in all these things you are more than conquerors through him who loved us. For I am convinced that neither death nor life, neither angels nor demons, neither the present nor the future, nor any powers, neither height nor depth, nor anything else in all creation, will be able to separate us from the love of God that is in Christ Jesus your Lord."

This powerful passage reminds you that nothing can separate you from the love of God. You are more than conquerors through Christ, and His love is constant and unwavering. Knowing that you are loved by the Creator of the universe helps to dispel insecurity and fills you with confidence.

As you meditate on these and other truths found in the Bible, you can replace the lies of insecurity with the truth of who you are in Christ. Embracing God's truth strengthens your identity and diminishes the power of insecurity in your lives. So, let's dive into His Word, allowing it to shape your thoughts and transform your perspective, empowering you to walk confidently in His love and purpose for us.

Section 3: Confronting the Lies

Insecurity often stems from believing lies about yourself. These lies may come from the enemy, other people, or even your own negative self-talk. But as followers of Christ, you have the power to confront and overcome these lies by standing on the truth of God's Word.

The Bible tells you that you are fearfully and wonderfully made (Psalm 139:14). God intentionally created you with purpose and value. You are not accidents or mistakes. Knowing this truth helps you combat feelings of worthlessness and insecurity. You can remind yourself that you are precious in God's eyes.

Moreover, God's love for you is unconditional. In Romans 8:38-39, it says that nothing can separate you from the love of God in Christ Jesus. No matter what you have done or what others may say about us, God's love remains steadfast. When you embrace this truth, it replaces the lies that say you are unlovable or unworthy.

God has also equipped you with unique gifts and talents. In 1 Peter 4:10, it says that you should use whatever gift you have received to serve others. You are not meant to compare yourself to others or feel inadequate. Instead, you can embrace the truth that God has given you specific abilities and passions to make a difference in the world.

Whenever negative thoughts or lies arise, you can combat them with the truth of God's Word. You can meditate on verses that remind you of your worth, identity, and purpose. By consistently aligning your thoughts with the truth, you can break free from the grip of insecurity and step into the confidence that comes from knowing who you are in Christ.

Confronting the lies that fuel insecurity is crucial for your growth and confidence as believers. By replacing those lies with the truth of God's Word, you can embrace your worth, bask in God's unconditional love, and utilize your unique gifts and talents. Remember to continuously meditate on the truth, rely on God's promises, and seek His guidance in your journey to overcome insecurity and walk confidently in His purpose for your lives.

Section 4: Seeking Validation from God

Insecurity can lead you to seek validation from others, always longing for their approval and acceptance. But it's essential to remember that true validation comes from God alone. In the Bible, you can find many verses that remind you of God's love and His affirmation of your worth.

In Psalm 139:14, it says, "I praise you because I am fearfully and wonderfully made; your works are wonderful, I know that full well." This verse reminds you that God created you uniquely and wonderfully. You don't need to seek validation from others because God has already declared your worth.

In Isaiah 43:4, God says, "You are precious in my eyes, and honored, and I love you." These words from God show you that you are valuable and loved in His sight. His opinion of you matters far more than what anyone else may think.

When you seek validation from God, you find a love that

surpasses all human understanding. God's love for you is unconditional, constant, and unchanging. In Romans 8:38-39, it says, "For I am convinced that neither death nor life, neither angels nor demons, neither the present nor the future, nor any powers, neither height nor depth, nor anything else in all creation, will be able to separate us from the love of God that is in Christ Jesus your Lord." This verse assures you that nothing can separate you from God's love.

When you find your validation in God, your insecurities begin to fade away. You can rest in the assurance that you are accepted and loved just as you are. You don't need to prove yourself to anyone because you have already been validated by the One who matters the most.

So, instead of seeking validation from others, seek God's affirmation and find your worth in His love. Spend time in prayer and meditate on His Word. Allow His truth to shape your identity and give you confidence. Remember, you are fearfully and wonderfully made, precious in His sight, and deeply loved by Him. Seek validation from God, and you will find the true and lasting acceptance your heart longs for.

Section 5: Cultivating a Grateful Heart

Insecurity often blinds you to the blessings and gifts you have been given. You tend to focus on what you lack and compare yourself to others, which only deepens your feelings of inadequacy. However, cultivating a grateful heart can transform your perspective and bring you closer to God.

The Bible encourages you to give thanks in all circumstances (1 Thessalonians 5:18). When you pause to count your blessings, you begin to see how God has provided for you in ways you may have overlooked. You realize that you are not alone in your struggles and that God is actively working in your lives.

Expressing gratitude to God is a powerful act of faith. It acknowledges His goodness, mercy, and love. It reminds you of His faithfulness in both the big and small things. By offering your thanks, you shift your focus from your insecurities to the abundant blessings that surround us.

Psalm 100:4 says, "Enter his gates with thanksgiving and his courts with praise; give thanks to him and praise his name." When you approach God with a grateful heart, you enter into His presence with joy and humility. Your hearts are lifted, and your perspective is transformed.

Gratitude also helps you to trust in God's provision. When you recognize His faithfulness in the past, you can have confidence in His provision for the future. In Philippians 4:6, you are encouraged to present your requests to God with thanksgiving. This act of gratitude aligns your hearts with God's will and strengthens your trust in His plan.

Cultivating a grateful heart is a daily practice. It requires intentional reflection and recognition of God's blessings. Start by keeping a gratitude journal, where you write down things you are thankful for each day. Take time to thank God in prayer, specifically acknowledging His goodness and provision.

As you develop a habit of gratitude, you will find that your insecurities begin to fade. You will realize that you are uniquely loved and cared for by a faithful God. Your perspective will shift, and you will find contentment in God's provision, rather than comparing yourself to others.

Remember, cultivating a grateful heart is not about denying challenges or pretending that everything is perfect. It is about acknowledging God's presence in the midst of difficulties and finding reasons to be thankful. By shifting your focus from insecurity to gratitude, you will experience a deeper sense of peace, contentment, and security in God's love and provision.

So, take a moment today to count your blessings and express gratitude to God. Cultivate a grateful heart and allow His love and provision to fill your life.

Section 6: Surrounding Yourself with Encouragement

Insecurity can be a tough battle to face, but you don't have to face it alone. Surrounding yourself with the right people can make a big difference. Look for friends who speak words of encouragement, love, and acceptance. Choose relationships that reflect God's heart and His desire for you to flourish.

In the Bible, in Proverbs 13:20, it says, "Walk with the wise and become wise, for a companion of fools suffers harm." This verse reminds you of the importance of choosing your companions wisely. When you spend time with people who uplift you and reminds you of your worth, it helps you grow in wisdom and confidence.

God designed you for community, and He wants you to be part of a supportive and uplifting environment. In 1 Thessalonians 5:11, it says, "Therefore encourage one another and build each other up, just as in fact you are doing." This verse shows you that encouragement is not only beneficial but also a commandment from God.

Surrounding yourself with positive influences doesn't mean you won't face challenges or insecurities, but it does mean you'll have a support system to help you through them. When you have friends who remind you of your identity in Christ and who encourage you to pursue your God-given purpose, it becomes easier to combat insecurities.

Additionally, being part of a church community can provide a nurturing environment where you can grow in your faith and find encouragement. In Hebrews 10:24-25, it says, "And let us consider how you may spur one another on toward love and good deeds, not giving up meeting together, as some are in the habit of doing, but encouraging one another—and all the more as you see the Day approaching." Being part of a church family allows you to support and encourage one another in your journey of faith.

Surrounding yourself with encouragement also means being intentional about the media you consume. Choose to engage with content that builds you up and aligns with your values. Limit exposure to negative messages or unrealistic standards that can feed into feelings of insecurity. Instead, seek out resources and media that remind you of your worth in God's eyes.

Remember, God created you uniquely and loves you unconditionally. Surround yourself with people and influences that reflect His love and acceptance. As you cultivate a community of encouragement, you will find strength, confidence, and a deeper understanding of your identity in Christ.

Section 7: Anchoring Your Identity in God's Love

The foundation of your identity lies in God's love for us. The Bible tells you in 1 John 4:16, "So you have come to know and to believe the love that God has for us. God is love, and anyone who abides in love abides in God, and God abides in them." This truth is a powerful reminder of your worth and significance in God's eyes.

God's love is unconditional and unchanging. It is not

based on your performance or external factors. Romans 5:8 assures us, "But God demonstrates his own love for us in this: While you were still sinners, Christ died for us." Even in your brokenness and imperfections, God loves you completely.

When feelings of insecurity or self-doubt arise, you can turn to God's love as your anchor. His love is steadfast and unwavering. It provides a solid foundation upon which you can build your identity. Ephesians 2:10 says, "For you are God's handiwork, created in Christ Jesus to do good works, which God prepared in advance for you to do." you are His masterpiece, uniquely designed and loved by Him.

As you anchor your identity in God's love, you find security and confidence. You no longer need to seek validation or approval from the world. Instead, you can rest in the assurance that you are deeply loved and accepted by your Heavenly Father.

Remind yourself daily of God's love for you. Fill your mind with His promises and truths found in Scripture. Psalm 139:14 declares, "I praise you because I am fearfully and wonderfully made; your works are wonderful, I know that full well." Embrace your uniqueness and value as a beloved child of God.

When the storms of life come, and doubts try to shake your identity, cling to God's love. Hebrews 6:19 describes it as an anchor for your souls, firm and secure. Just as an anchor keeps a ship steady amidst turbulent waters, God's love keeps you grounded and unshakable.

In moments of weakness, remember the words of 2 Corinthians 12:9, "But he said to me, 'My grace is sufficient for you, for my power is made perfect in weakness.'" God's love is greater than any insecurity or doubt you may feel. His grace empowers you to overcome and grow stronger in Him.

So, anchor your identity in God's love. Embrace the truth that you are loved beyond measure, chosen, and cherished. Let His love be the foundation from which you live, love, and impact the world. Rest in the security of His unfailing love, for it is in Him that you find your truest identity.

Section 8: Stepping Out in Faith

Insecurity often holds you back and keeps you from taking steps of faith. You may feel unsure of yourself or doubt your abilities. But as followers of Christ, you are called to live with boldness and courage. The Bible tells you in Joshua 1:9, "Be strong and courageous. Do not be afraid; do not be discouraged, for the Lord your God will be with you wherever you go."

When you strengthen your identity in Christ, you can overcome insecurity and step out in faith. Remember that your worth and value come from God, not from the opinions of others. He has uniquely equipped you with gifts and talents for His purposes. Take comfort in Psalm 139:14, which says, "I praise you because I am fearfully and wonderfully made; your works are wonderful, I know that full well."

As you step out of your comfort zone, be open to the opportunities God places before you. It may involve trying something new, speaking up for what is right, or sharing your faith with others. Even if you feel inadequate or uncertain, trust that God will equip and empower you. Philippians 4:13 reminds us, "I can do all things through Christ who strengthens me."

Remember the story of Moses in Exodus 3 and 4. When God called Moses to lead the Israelites out of Egypt, Moses felt insecure and doubted himself. But God assured Moses that He would be with him and provide what he needed. In the same way, God is with you as you step out in faith. He will guide you and give you the strength to overcome any insecurities or obstacles.

Stepping out in faith requires trust and reliance on God. Proverbs 3:5-6 encourages us, "Trust in the Lord with all your heart and lean not on your own understanding; in all your ways submit to him, and he will make your paths straight." When you surrender your fears and insecurities to God, He will guide your steps and make a way for you.

As you take those steps of faith, remember that even if things don't go as planned, God is still in control. Romans 8:28 reminds us, "And you know that in all things God works for the good of those who love him, who have been called according to his purpose." Trust that God can turn any situation, even the challenging ones, for your ultimate good and His glory.

Stepping out in faith requires overcoming insecurity and trusting in God's guidance and provision. Strengthen your identity in Christ and remember that He has equipped you for His purposes. Take courage and embrace the opportunities before you, knowing that God is with you every step of the way. Step out in faith, relying on His strength, and watch as He works in and through you to accomplish great things for His kingdom.

Section 9: Overcoming Comparison

Comparison is a sneaky trap that can lead to feelings of insecurity. In today's world, it's so easy to look at other people's lives, accomplishments, and looks and feel like we're not good enough. But here's the thing: God made you special and unique. He created you with your own special talents and purposes. So instead of comparing yourself to others, let's focus on your own journey.

The Bible reminds you in Psalm 139:14 that you are fearfully and wonderfully made by God. He crafted every part of you with care and intention. Your worth doesn't come from how you measure up to others; it comes from being a beloved child of God.

When you find yourself tempted to compare, you can turn to God's Word for guidance. Galatians 6:4-5 encourages you to "pay careful attention to [our] own work, for then [we] will get the satisfaction of a job well done, and [we] won't need to compare [ourselves] to anyone else." God wants you to focus on your own path and celebrate the successes of others without feeling inferior.

Comparing yourself to others only brings discontentment and steals your joy. Instead, let's redirect your thoughts to gratitude. Let's be thankful for who God made you to be and the unique gifts He has given us. When you embrace your own identity and purpose, you can find fulfillment and live a life that brings glory to God.

So, the next time you catch yourself comparing, remember that you are fearfully and wonderfully made. Take a moment to thank God for who you are and the purpose He has for your life. Celebrate the successes of others without allowing them to diminish your own worth. Trust that God has a plan for you, and He will use your unique qualities to make a difference in the world.

Remember, you are loved, valued, and irreplaceable in God's eyes. Embrace your identity in Christ and live confidently, knowing that you are exactly who God created you to be.

Section 10: Connecting with a Supportive Community

Connecting with a supportive community is vital in overcoming challenges and persevering in faith. In the Bible, you are encouraged to gather together and support one another. Hebrews 10:24-25 says, "And let us consider how you may spur one another on toward love and good deeds, not giving up meeting together, as some are in the habit of doing, but encouraging one another—and all the more as you see the Day approaching."

Surrounding yourself with a community of believers provides a safe space where you can share your struggles and victories without judgment. When you engage in a local church or join small groups, you'll find like-minded individuals who understand your journey and can offer support, encouragement, and prayers. They can remind you of your worth and potential when you're feeling insecure or discouraged.

In Ecclesiastes 4:9-10, it says, "Two are better than one because they have a good return for their labor: If either of them falls down, one can help the other up. But pity anyone who falls and has no one to help them up." Having a supportive community means you don't have to face challenges alone. You can lean on your brothers and sisters in Christ, sharing burdens, and finding strength in unity.

Moreover, being part of a supportive community provides accountability. James 5:16 encourages you to confess your sins to one another and pray for each other so that you may be healed. When you have trusted friends who hold you accountable, you can grow stronger in your faith and overcome challenges together. They can offer guidance, wisdom, and gentle correction when needed.

Jesus Himself set an example of the importance of

community by gathering disciples and sharing life with them. They encouraged and challenged one another, and they became a close-knit community that supported each other through thick and thin.

Connecting with a supportive community is crucial in overcoming challenges and persevering in faith. It provides a place where you can find encouragement, accountability, and understanding. Seek out a local church or small groups where you can build relationships with like-minded believers. Together, you can uplift one another, share burdens, and find strength in unity. Remember, you don't have to face challenges alone. God has provided a community of believers to walk alongside you on your journey of faith.

Wrap Up

Battling insecurity and strengthening your identity in Christ is a journey that requires intentionality and a reliance on God's truth. Embrace the truth of who you are in Christ and confront the lies that breed insecurity. Seek validation from God alone and cultivate a grateful heart. Surround yourself with positive influences and anchor your identity in God's love. Step out in faith, knowing that God has equipped you to overcome insecurity and walk confidently in His plan for your life. Remember, you are fearfully and wonderfully made, and your identity in Christ is unshakable.

CHAPTER 8

THE BROTHERHOOD: NAVIGATING RELATIONSHIPS WITH GODLY INFLUENCE

BROTHERHOOD IS important for navigating relationships with godly influence. Surrounding yourself with the right kind of friendships and mentors is vital for your spiritual growth and development. Together, you will delve into the power of godly relationships and discover how they can shape and impact your life.

Section 1: The Power of Relationships

The Bible reminds you of the power of relationships and the importance of choosing your companions wisely. In Proverbs 13:20, it says, "Walk with the wise and become wise, for a companion of fools suffers harm." When you surround yourself with godly individuals who are seeking to live according to God's principles, you are more likely to grow in wisdom and faith.

In 1 Corinthians 15:33, it warns us, "Do not be misled: 'Bad company corrupts good character.'" This verse serves as a reminder that your relationships can either build you up or lead you astray. You should seek friendships that encourage you in your walk with God, challenge you to grow, and hold you accountable.

Additionally, Ecclesiastes 4:9-10 highlights the strength and support that comes from having godly relationships: "Two are better than one because they have a good return for their labor: If either of them falls down, one can help the other up. But pity anyone who falls and has no one to help them up." When you have strong relationships with fellow believers, you can lean on each other during difficult times, providing support, encouragement, and prayer.

Jesus Himself emphasized the importance of loving one another and being united as His followers. In John 13:34-35, He says, "A new command I give you: Love one another. As I have loved you, so you must love one another. By this everyone will know that you are my disciples if you love one another." your relationships should reflect the love of Christ and serve as a testimony to the world.

Therefore, be intentional in building and nurturing relationships that draw you closer to God. Seek out fellow believers who can mentor and encourage you in your faith journey. Surround yourself with friends who inspire you to live a life pleasing to God. Pray for wisdom and discernment in choosing your companions, and always strive to be a positive influence on others.

Remember, the power of relationships is immense. Choose friendships that align with your values, support your spiritual growth, and ultimately bring glory to God. By investing in godly relationships, you create a strong foundation for overcoming challenges and persevering in faith.

Section 2: Choosing Godly Influences

In your journey of understanding God's plan for your lives, it is crucial to be mindful of the influences you allow into your lives. The people you spend time with can have a significant impact on your spiritual growth and development. The Bible reminds you of the importance of choosing godly influences.

Proverbs 13:20 says, "Walk with the wise and become wise, for a companion of fools suffers harm." This verse emphasizes the importance of surrounding yourself with wise and godly individuals who can guide you in your faith journey. When you choose friends and mentors who share your beliefs and values, they can support us, encourage us, and help you stay on the right path.

1 Corinthians 15:33 warns, "Do not be misled: 'Bad company corrupts good character.'" It reminds you that spending time with people who do not honor God can negatively impact your character and lead you astray. Therefore, it is essential to be discerning about the company you keep and the influences you allow into your lives.

Seek out friendships and mentors who are committed to their relationship with God. Look for individuals who exemplify godly character, integrity, and a genuine love for others. Surrounding yourself with such people can provide you with positive role models and a strong support system.

Hebrews 10:24-25 encourages you to "consider how you may spur one another on toward love and good deeds, not giving up meeting together, as some are in the habit of doing." This verse highlights the importance of gathering with fellow believers to encourage and uplift one another. Participating in a church community or small group can provide opportunities to build relationships with like-minded individuals who can help you grow spiritually.

Choosing godly influences does not mean isolating yourself from the world but rather being intentional about the relationships you cultivate. It means seeking out friends and mentors who will inspire you to pursue God's plans, challenge you to live according to His Word, and help you become the best version of yourself .

As you choose godly influences, strive to be a godly influence on others. Share your faith, demonstrate Christ's love, and encourage those around you to draw closer to God. Together, you can create a supportive and uplifting community that fosters spiritual growth and empowers you to impact the world for Christ.

Choosing godly influences is essential for your spiritual growth. Surrounding yourself with individuals who share your faith and values can positively impact your character, help you stay on the right path, and provide you with a strong support system. Seek out friendships and mentors who inspire you to pursue God's plans and challenge you to live according to His Word. By choosing godly influences and being intentional about your relationships, you can grow in your understanding of

God's plan for your life and make a lasting impact on the world.

Section 3: The Importance of Accountability

Accountability is incredibly important in your journey of faith. It's like having a teammate who helps you stay focused and accountable to God's ways. In the Bible, Proverbs 27:17 says, "As iron sharpens iron, so one person sharpens another." This verse reminds you that you need others to challenge and encourage you on your path.

When you have someone who holds you accountable, you have an extra layer of support. They can help you recognize when you make mistakes or stray from God's plan. Just like a loving coach, they can gently point out areas where you need to improve and guide you back to the right path.

Having accountability also helps you grow in your relationship with God. When you share your struggles and victories with someone you trust, they can pray for you and offer guidance. They can remind you of God's promises and help you see things from a different perspective.

In the book of Ecclesiastes, chapter 4, verse 9, it says, "Two are better than one because they have a good return for their labor." This verse emphasizes the power of partnership and accountability. When you have someone walking alongside us, you can accomplish more and overcome challenges together.

Finding a trusted friend or mentor to hold you accountable is essential. It should be someone who loves God and desires the best for us. This person will listen without judgment, offer wise counsel, and pray for us. They will keep you focused on your purpose and remind you of your identity in Christ.

As you journey through life, accountability keeps you on the right track. It's not about someone trying to control us, but rather about having a loving companion who helps you become the best version of yourself . So, let's seek accountability, embrace it with gratitude, and be willing to be accountable to others too. Together, you can grow stronger in your faith and make wise choices that honor God.

Section 4: Building Healthy Relationships

Building strong and healthy relationships takes work and being intentional. It begins by being a good friend yourself, which means being kind, supportive, and someone others can trust. It's important to listen to others with care and try to understand where they're coming from. Treat others the way you would like to be treated. When relationships are built on respect, trust, and love, they become healthy and strong.

In the Bible, Proverbs 17:17 says, "A friend loves at all times, and a brother is born for a time of adversity." This reminds you that true friendship is there for you through thick and thin, supporting you during difficult times. In John

15:13, Jesus says, "Greater love has no one than this: to lay down one's life for one's friends." This shows you the ultimate example of love and sacrifice, teaching you to care for your friends deeply.

Remember, building healthy relationships is a lifelong journey, and it starts with being a good friend yourself.

As you continue to build healthy relationships, it's essential to practice effective communication. Communication involves expressing your thoughts and feelings clearly and respectfully, while also listening attentively to others. When you communicate well, you can avoid misunderstandings and conflicts.

In the Bible, Proverbs 18:13 states, "To answer before listening—that is folly and shame." This verse emphasizes the importance of actively listening before responding. By listening carefully, you can understand others better and respond in a way that promotes understanding and harmony.

Another key aspect of building healthy relationships is forgiveness. No one is perfect, and you all make mistakes. It's important to be willing to forgive others when they hurt you and to seek forgiveness when you have done wrong. Ephesians 4:32 encourages us, saying, "Be kind and compassionate to one another, forgiving each other, just as in Christ God forgave you."

Building healthy relationships also means setting boundaries. Boundaries are guidelines that help protect your well-being and maintain healthy dynamics in relationships.

It's okay to say no when something doesn't feel right or when it goes against your values. In the book of Galatians 5:13, it is written, "You, my brothers and sisters, were called to be free. But do not use your freedom to indulge the flesh; rather, serve one another humbly in love." This verse reminds you that setting boundaries is an act of self-care and allows you to love and serve others in a healthy way.

Finally, remember that building healthy relationships requires patience and understanding. People are unique, and conflicts may arise. Instead of reacting impulsively, seek, to understand the other person's perspective and find common ground. Romans 12:18 advises, "If it is possible, as far as it depends on you, live at peace with everyone." This verse encourages you to strive for peace and harmony in your relationships, doing your part to maintain healthy connections.

In summary, building healthy relationships involves being a good friend, practicing effective communication, forgiving others, setting boundaries, and being patient and understanding. By following these principles and drawing wisdom from the Bible, you can cultivate strong and fulfilling relationships in your life.

Section 5: Being a Light in Relationships

As a follower of Christ, you have the opportunity to be a light in your relationships. The Bible tells you in Matthew

5:16, "Let your light shine before others, that they may see your good deeds and glorify your Father in heaven." This means that through your actions and words, you can reflect the love and grace of Jesus to those around us.

In your relationships, you can show kindness and understanding. When someone is going through a difficult time, be there to offer a listening ear and a comforting presence. Offer words of encouragement and support, reminding them of God's faithfulness and love. In Colossians 3:12, you are encouraged to clothe yourself with compassion, kindness, humility, gentleness, and patience. By doing so, you demonstrate the character of Christ in your interactions.

Forgiveness is also crucial in your relationships. Ephesians 4:32 reminds you to "be kind and compassionate to one another, forgiving each other, just as in Christ God forgave you." When conflicts arise, choose to extend forgiveness, and seek reconciliation. Let go of grudges and bitterness and strive to restore harmony in your relationships.

Being a light means showing genuine love and care to others. In John 13:34-35, Jesus said, "A new command I give you: Love one another. As I have loved you, so you must love one another. By this everyone will know that you are my disciples if you love one another." Let your love for others be a reflection of Christ's love for us. Love sacrificially, unconditionally, and without expecting anything in return.

In your relationships, be a source of hope. Point others to Jesus and the hope found in Him. Share your faith with gentleness and respect when appropriate. Let your actions speak louder than words and allow your Christ-like character to draw others closer to God.

Remember, being a light in your relationships doesn't mean you have to be perfect. You all make mistakes and fall short at times. But it's in those moments that you can humble yourself , seek forgiveness, and demonstrate grace. Allow God's love to shine through your imperfections and be open to growing and learning in your relationships.

In conclusion, as a follower of Christ, you have the privilege and responsibility to be a light in your relationships. Show kindness, forgiveness, and compassion. Be a source of encouragement and support. Let your actions and words reflect the love and grace of Jesus. Through your Christ-like character, you can impact and inspire others, ultimately bringing glory to your Heavenly Father.

Section 6: Seeking Godly Mentors

Mentors are like spiritual guides who can help you navigate your journey of faith. They have walked the path before you and can offer valuable insights and wisdom based on their own experiences. The Bible encourages you to seek out mentors who can provide godly counsel and guidance.

In the book of Proverbs, it says, "Listen to advice and accept instruction, that you may gain wisdom in the future"

(Proverbs 19:20). Godly mentors can offer advice and instruction that can help you grow in wisdom and understanding.

When choosing a mentor, look for someone who demonstrates godly character and a deep understanding of the Word of God. Seek out individuals who have a genuine love for God and a passion for His truth. Their life should align with biblical principles and reflect the fruits of the Spirit.

In the New Testament, the apostle Paul serves as an example of a mentor. He took Timothy under his wing and mentored him in the ways of the faith. Paul wrote to Timothy, "You, however, have followed my teaching, my conduct, my aim in life, my faith, my patience, my love, my steadfastness" (2 Timothy 3:10). Timothy learned from Paul's example and teachings, and it had a profound impact on his own ministry.

Having a mentor allows you to benefit from their wisdom, guidance, and prayers. They can help you navigate challenges, offer practical advice, and hold you accountable in your walk with God. A mentor can provide encouragement and support during difficult times and celebrate your growth and victories.

The relationship with a mentor is built on trust and mutual respect. It is essential to approach this relationship with a humble and teachable heart. Be open to receiving correction and guidance, knowing that it comes from a place of love and a desire to see you grow in your faith.

Remember, finding a mentor is not about finding a perfect

person, but someone who can point you to the perfect God. Mentors are not infallible, but they can provide valuable insights and share their experiences of God's faithfulness.

If you do not currently have a mentor, seek guidance from your church community or Christian organizations. Pray and ask God to lead you to the right person. Be willing to invest time and effort into the mentorship relationship, recognizing the mutual benefits it brings.

Seeking godly mentors is a wise decision on your journey of faith. Mentors can offer guidance, wisdom, and accountability as you seek to grow closer to God. Choose mentors who exhibit godly character and possess a deep understanding of the Word of God. Embrace the mentorship relationship with humility and openness and allow God to use it to shape and transform your life.

Section 7: Growing Together in Christ

Godly relationships are not just about receiving but also giving. When you are part of a community of believers, you have the opportunity to grow together in Christ. Engage in small groups, Bible studies, or fellowship with like-minded individuals. Share your struggles, victories, and faith journeys. Pray for one another and support each other in the highs and lows of life.

In the book of Acts, you see the early Christians gathering together, devoting themselves to the teachings of the apostles, fellowship, breaking of bread, and prayer (Acts 2:42). They understood the importance of growing together in Christ and building each other up. Similarly, the apostle Paul encourages the believers in Hebrews 10:24-25 to spur one another on toward love and good deeds, not neglecting to meet together.

When you come together with fellow believers, you find encouragement, accountability, and spiritual nourishment. Proverbs 27:17 reminds you that, "Iron sharpens iron, and one man sharpens another." Through meaningful relationships, you can sharpen and strengthen your faith.

As you grow together in Christ, you can learn from one another's experiences and wisdom. You can offer support, guidance, and a listening ear to those who are going through challenges. Galatians 6:2 instructs you to "Bear one another's burdens, and so fulfill the law of Christ."

Additionally, when you share your own struggles and victories, you create an atmosphere of authenticity and vulnerability. You realize that you are not alone in your journey and that others can relate to your experiences. James 5:16 encourages you to confess your sins to one another and pray for each other, so that you may be healed.

Prayer is a vital aspect of growing together in Christ. When you pray for one another, you intercede on behalf of your brothers and sisters in Christ. You lift up their needs, seeking God's guidance, comfort, and provision. Philippians 4:6 reminds us, "Do not be anxious about anything, but in every situation, by prayer and petition, with thanksgiving, present your requests to God."

As you grow together in Christ, you also spur each other on toward love and good deeds. You encourage one another to live out your faith in practical ways, showing love and kindness to those around us. Hebrews 10:24 encourages you to "consider how you may spur one another on toward love and good deeds."

Growing together in Christ is a beautiful and essential part of your spiritual journey. When you engage in meaningful relationships with fellow believers, you have the opportunity to learn, encourage, and support one another. Through prayer, fellowship, and sharing your faith journeys, you can grow in your love for God and others. Embrace the power of community and seek to grow together in Christ, knowing that you are stronger and more impactful when you walk together in faith.

Section 8: Grace in Relationships

No relationship is perfect. You all make mistakes, and conflicts may arise. In these moments, it's crucial to extend grace and forgiveness to one another, just as God has extended His grace and forgiveness to us.

The Bible teaches you about the importance of grace in relationships. In Colossians 3:13, it says, "Bear with each other and forgive one another if any of you has a grievance against someone. Forgive as the Lord forgave you." This verse reminds you that just as God has forgiven you of your sins, you should also forgive others.

When you choose to extend grace, you show compassion, understanding, and empathy. You recognize that you are all imperfect and in need of forgiveness. Ephesians 4:32 encourages you to, "Be kind and compassionate to one another, forgiving each other, just as in Christ God forgave you."

Grace also involves communication. Proverbs 15:1 reminds you that, "A gentle answer turns away wrath, but a harsh word stirs up anger." When conflicts arise, you should approach each other with gentleness and humility, seeking to understand and resolve the issues at hand.

Sometimes, relationships may become strained or broken. However, through grace and forgiveness, you can work towards reconciliation and restoration. Matthew 18:21-22 teaches you about the importance of forgiveness, "Then Peter came to Jesus and asked, 'Lord, how many times shall I forgive my brother or sister who sins against me? Up to seven times?' Jesus answered, 'I tell you, not seven times, but seventy-seven times.'"

In extending grace to one another, you emulate the love and forgiveness that God has shown us. You recognize that you are all on a journey of growth and transformation. By offering grace, love, and forgiveness, relationships can be strengthened and deepened, fostering an environment of trust, understanding, and acceptance.

As you navigate your relationships, remember the power of grace. Choose to forgive, communicate with kindness, and seek reconciliation. Allow God's grace to flow through you, bringing healing and restoration to your relationships. Remember the words of Romans 12:18, "If it is possible, as far as it depends on you, live at peace with everyone." Let grace be the foundation of your relationships, allowing God's love to shine through your interactions with others.

Section 9: Fostering Unity and Harmony

In your relationships, it is vital to foster unity and harmony. As believers, you are called to be peacemakers and to promote unity among fellow brothers and sisters in Christ. Strive to resolve conflicts in a spirit of love and humility. Seek reconciliation and work towards understanding one another. Embrace diversity and appreciate the unique perspectives and gifts that each individual brings. Together, you can create a community that reflects the love and unity of Christ.

The Bible reminds you in Romans 12:18, "If it is possible, as far as it depends on you, live at peace with everyone." God desires for His children to live in harmony and unity, as it reflects His character and His plan for His people. In Ephesians 4:3, you are urged to make every effort to maintain the unity of the Spirit in the bond of peace.

Jesus Himself prayed for unity among His followers in John 17:21, saying, "...that all of them may be one, Father, just as you are in me and I am in you. May they also be in you so that the world may believe that you have sent me." your unity and love for one another are powerful testimonies to the world of God's love and presence among us.

To foster unity, you must cultivate a heart of forgiveness and grace. Ephesians 4:32 encourages you to be kind and compassionate, forgiving one another, just as God forgave you in Christ. Let go of grudges and resentments and extend forgiveness to those who have wronged you. Through forgiveness, you break down barriers and create opportunities for healing and reconciliation.

In your interactions, let you practice active listening and empathy. James 1:19 advises you to be quick to listen, slow to speak, and slow to become angry. Seek to understand the perspectives and feelings of others, even if they differ from your own. Value each person's worth and dignity as a child of God, regardless of differences in background or opinions.

Promoting unity also involves embracing diversity. God has intentionally created each person with unique talents, abilities, and experiences. Romans 12:4-5 reminds you that you are all part of one body, with different functions. Embrace the beauty of diversity and celebrate the gifts that others bring. Learn from one another and grow together as you work towards a common purpose.

In fostering unity, remember that it is not solely your

efforts but the work of the Holy Spirit in your midst. Galatians 5:22-23 reminds you of the fruit of the Spirit, which includes love, joy, peace, patience, kindness, goodness, faithfulness, gentleness, and self-control. Allow the Holy Spirit to guide your interactions and relationships, enabling you to exhibit these qualities that foster unity.

Commit yourself to fostering unity and harmony within your communities, churches, and families. Through your love, humility, forgiveness, and appreciation of diversity, you can create an environment where the love of Christ shines brightly. By living in unity, you reflect the character of God and become agents of transformation in a divided world.

Section 10: Encouraging Spiritual Growth

Godly relationships are a catalyst for spiritual growth. Surrounding yourself with like-minded individuals who are passionate about their faith can inspire and challenge you to grow deeper in your relationship with God. Engage in meaningful conversations about faith, share insights from Scripture, and encourage one another in pursuing a life that honors God. By spurring one another on towards spiritual maturity, you will experience personal growth and help others do the same.

In the Bible, the book of Proverbs tells us, "Iron sharpens iron, and one man sharpens another" (Proverbs 27:17). This verse reminds you of the importance of having supportive relationships that sharpen and strengthen your faith. Just as iron blades become sharper when they rub against each other, you too can grow in your faith when you interact with fellow believers.

Jesus emphasized the significance of gathering together as believers, saying, "For where two or three are gathered in my name, there am I among them" (Matthew 18:20). When you come together in His name, God's presence is with us, and your faith is strengthened. You can learn from one another's experiences, gain fresh perspectives on Scripture, and encourage each other in your walk with God.

The apostle Paul, in his letters to various churches, often expressed his gratitude for the faith and spiritual growth of fellow believers. He encouraged them to continue growing in their knowledge and understanding of God. In his letter to the Colossians, he wrote, "Therefore, as you received Christ Jesus the Lord, so walk in him, rooted and built up in him and established in the faith" (Colossians 2:6-7).

Accountability is another vital aspect of fostering spiritual growth. Having trusted friends who can lovingly challenge and hold you accountable helps you stay on track in your faith journey. They can gently point out areas where you may need to grow or areas where you may be straying from God's path.

Hebrews 10:24-25 encourages us, "And let us consider how to stir up one another to love and good works, not neglecting to meet together, as is the habit of some, but encouraging one another, and all the more as you see the Day drawing near."

This verse emphasizes the importance of gathering regularly as a community of believers to encourage one another and spur each other on in acts of love and good deeds.

As you cultivate relationships that prioritize spiritual growth, remember to be intentional in seeking out opportunities for fellowship, such as joining a small group, attending Bible studies, or serving together in ministry. By investing in these relationships, you can create an environment where spiritual growth flourishes, and together, you can encourage one another to live lives that bring glory to God.

Wrap Up

Surrounding yourself with godly relationships is essential for spiritual growth. Engage in meaningful conversations, share insights from Scripture, and encourage one another to pursue a life that honors God. As iron sharpens iron, you can sharpen and strengthen your faith through these relationships. Seek out accountability and be intentional in fostering a community that prioritizes spiritual growth. By spurring one another on in faith, you will experience personal growth and collectively become a powerful force for God's kingdom.

CHAPTER 9
IMPACTING THE WORLD: STEPPING INTO YOUR GOD-GIVEN MISSION

WHAT DIFFERENCE CAN I MAKE? That's a great question and one that has inspired so many to do amazing things. Let's look at how you can make a positive impact on the world around you. God has given you a unique mission, and by embracing it, you can contribute to His kingdom and bring about transformation. Let's discover how you can step into your God-given mission and make a difference in the world.

Section 1: Unleashing Your Potential

Did you know that God created you with unique talents, passions, and gifts? He designed you with a purpose in mind, and He has equipped you to fulfill that purpose. The Bible tells you in Ephesians 2:10, "For you are God's handiwork, created in Christ Jesus to do good works, which God prepared in advance for us to do."

Take some time to reflect on your strengths and areas of interest. What are you naturally good at? What activities bring you joy and fulfillment? These can be clues to uncovering your God-given potential.

Consider how you can use your talents and passions to make a positive impact on others. Maybe you have a gift for music, and you can use your voice or instruments to bring joy and inspire others. Or perhaps you have a knack for teaching, and you can share your knowledge and wisdom to help others grow. Whatever your strengths may be, there is a way for you to use them to make a difference.

Remember the parable of the talents in Matthew 25:14-30. The master gave each servant talents, and those who used them wisely were commended. Similarly, when you embrace your potential and use your gifts for God's purposes, you become a powerful force for good in the world.

Don't be afraid to step out of your comfort zone and try new things. God often stretches you beyond what you think we're capable of, and He empowers you to accomplish great things. In Philippians 4:13, you are reminded, "I can do all this through him who gives me strength."

Seek God's guidance and ask Him to reveal His plans for you. Spend time in prayer, asking Him to show you how you can use your potential to bring glory to His name. As you align your life with His purposes, you will experience a deep sense of fulfillment and joy.

Remember, you are fearfully and wonderfully made (Psalm 139:14). God has given you unique abilities and passions for a reason. Embrace your potential and step out in faith. As you do, you will unleash a powerful force of goodness and impact the world around you for God's kingdom.

Section 2: Serving Others

Serving others is at the heart of the Christian faith. In the Bible, Jesus teaches you the importance of serving those around us. In Mark 10:45, Jesus says, "For even the Son of Man did not come to be served, but to serve, and to give his life as a ransom for many." He lived a life of selflessness, constantly reaching out to those in need, healing the sick, and showing compassion to the marginalized.

As followers of Christ, you are called to follow His example and serve others with love and humility. In Matthew 25:40, Jesus says, "Truly I tell you, whatever you did for one of the least of these brothers and sisters of mine, you did for me." When you serve others, you are serving Jesus Himself.

Serving others doesn't always require grand gestures or extraordinary acts. It can be as simple as lending a helping hand to a neighbor, volunteering at a local charity, or even offering a kind word to someone in distress. Acts of service can make a significant impact on the lives of others, even if you may not realize it at the time.

Moreover, serving others is not just about meeting physical needs but also about showing compassion and empathy. Sometimes, people may be going through emotional or spiritual struggles, and a listening ear or a word of encouragement can provide immense comfort. Galatians 5:13 reminds us, "You, my brothers and sisters, were called to be free. But do not use your freedom to indulge the flesh; rather, serve one another humbly in love."

When you serve others, you reflect the love of Christ to the world. It becomes an opportunity to share God's grace and bring hope to those who may be feeling hopeless. By serving others, you can break down barriers, build bridges, and create a sense of community where everyone feels valued and loved.

As you go about your daily life, be attentive to the needs of those around you. Look for opportunities to serve, whether big or small. Pray and ask God to open your eyes to the needs that may be present in your community. Seek His guidance in how you can be of service to others.

Remember, serving others is not just a one-time event; it's

a lifestyle. It requires a heart that is willing to put others before oneself. By continually seeking ways to serve, you will not only impact the lives of others but also experience the joy and fulfillment that comes from living out your God-given purpose.

Serving others is a fundamental aspect of the Christian faith. Jesus showed you the way by His own example of selfless service. Follow in His footsteps, serving others with love, compassion, and humility. Whether through acts of kindness, volunteering, or lending a listening ear, every act of service matters. By serving others, you bring glory to God and make a positive impact on the world around us.

Section 3: Sharing God's Love

Sharing God's love is at the heart of your Christian faith. The Bible teaches you in John 3:16, "For God so loved the world that he gave his one and only Son, that whoever believes in him shall not perish but have eternal life." This incredible love that God has shown you is meant to be shared with others.

When you share your personal faith journey, you are providing a glimpse of God's transforming power in your lives. You can share how God has brought hope, healing, and restoration into your own stories. By being open and honest about your struggles and victories, you allow others to see the real-life impact of God's love.

Inviting others to church is another powerful way to share God's love. The church is a place where people can gather, worship, and learn about God's Word together. It is a community of believers who can support and encourage one another. By extending an invitation to someone, you provide them with an opportunity to experience God's love and find a spiritual home.

Engaging in conversations about faith is essential for sharing God's love. It can be as simple as having a genuine conversation with a friend or family member about your beliefs. By sharing your thoughts, answering questions, and listening to others' perspectives, you create a space for dialogue and reflection. Through these conversations, seeds of faith can be planted, and hearts can be opened to the love of God.

Participating in mission trips is another way to share God's love globally. Mission trips provide opportunities to serve and minister to people in different communities and cultures. It allows you to meet people where they are, show acts of kindness, and share the message of God's love. As you serve others, you become living testimonies of God's love in action.

Remember, impacting the world begins with sharing God's love one person at a time. Just as Jesus reached out to individuals and transformed their lives, you too can make a difference by sharing the love of Christ with those around us. Be bold and intentional in sharing your faith, knowing that God can use your efforts to bring eternal impact to others.

Section 4: Leading by Example

Leadership is not about having a fancy title or being in a high position. It's about showing others how to live in a way that honors God and positively impacts those around you. You don't have to be famous or well-known to be a leader. In fact, some of the most influential leaders are the ones who lead by example in their everyday lives.

When you lead by example, you live your life in a way that reflects the values and teachings of the Bible. You treat others with kindness, respect, and love, just as Jesus did. You show integrity by being honest and trustworthy in all that you do. Your actions match your words, and people can see that you genuinely care about others.

By leading with Godly values, you become a role model for those around you. Your family, friends, classmates, and colleagues notice how you live your life. They see your character and the way you handle challenges and difficult situations. Your positive attitude and humble heart inspire others to pursue God's plan for their own lives.

In the Bible, Jesus is the ultimate example of leadership. He taught his disciples how to serve others and love one another. Jesus washed his disciples' feet, showing them the importance of humility and serving others with a servant's heart. He showed compassion to those who were hurting and reached out to the marginalized and forgotten.

As a leader, you can follow Jesus' example by serving

others and treating them with compassion. Look for opportunities to help those in need, whether it's volunteering at a local shelter, lending a hand to a friend in need, or simply listening to someone who is going through a tough time. Your acts of kindness can make a big difference in someone's life.

When you lead by example, you create a ripple effect that can transform lives and communities. Your positive influence can inspire others to step up and make a difference too. As people see the love of Christ reflected in your actions, they may be drawn closer to God and inspired to live in a way that honors Him.

So, remember that you don't need a fancy title or position to be a leader. Leading by example starts with living a life that reflects God's love and teachings. Demonstrate integrity, compassion, and a servant's heart in all that you do. Be a role model for others and watch as your influence positively impacts those around you. Your leadership can be a powerful force for change in the world.

Section 5: Using Your Skills and Talents

God has given you unique skills and talents that are meant to be used for His glory. In the Bible, you can find examples of individuals who used their abilities to make a difference in the world. One such example is Bezalel, who was filled with the Spirit of God and given skills in craftsmanship and design (Exodus 31:1-5). Bezalel used his talents to help build the tabernacle, creating beautiful and intricate works of art.

Just like Bezalel, you have been gifted with specific skills and talents. Take some time to reflect on what you are good at and passionate about. Are you a talented writer, musician, or athlete? Maybe you have a knack for problem-solving, teaching, or encouraging others. These abilities are not accidents; they are part of God's plan for your life.

Consider how you can use your skills and talents to impact the world around you. If you are an artist, use your creativity to create artwork that inspires and uplifts others. Your paintings, sculptures, or music can be a source of hope and joy for those who experience them. If you are good at organizing, volunteer to help plan events that benefit your community or church. Your attention to detail and organizational skills can make a significant impact in bringing people together for a greater cause.

Remember, it's not about comparing your talents to others or seeking recognition. Instead, focus on using your unique abilities to serve others and bring glory to God. By using your skills and talents for God's purposes, you become a faithful steward of the gifts He has entrusted to you.

As you step out and use your abilities, trust that God will guide and empower you. Pray for wisdom and discernment in how to best utilize your talents. Seek opportunities where you can make a positive impact, whether it's within your family, church, school, or community. Even small acts done with a heart of love and faithfulness can create ripples of change in the world.

As you embark on this journey of using your skills and talents for God's purposes, remember that it's not about perfection or immediate results. It's about being faithful and obedient to what God has called you to do. Allow Him to work through you and use your unique abilities to bring about His kingdom on earth.

Your skills and talents are not meant to be hidden or wasted. They are gifts from God, given to you for a purpose. Embrace your abilities, seek ways to utilize them for God's glory, and make a positive impact on the world around you. Whether you are an artist, organizer, teacher, or any other skilled individual, let your light shine and bring hope, joy, and transformation to those who cross your path. Use your skills and talents to point others to the love and grace of your Creator.

Section 6: Praying for the World

Prayer is not just a simple act of talking to God; it is a powerful tool that can shape the world around us. When you pray, you communicate with your Heavenly Father, who is loving and compassionate. He listens to your prayers and desires to bring healing, transformation, and justice to the world.

In the Bible, you find numerous examples of the power of prayer. In James 5:16, it says, "The prayer of a righteous person is powerful and effective." your prayers have the ability to bring about real change in the lives of others and in the world at large.

When you pray for the world, you open yourself to God's heart and His concerns. You can pray for peace to prevail in places torn by conflict and violence. You can intercede for justice to be established, so that the oppressed may find relief and the downtrodden may experience freedom. Praying for healing allows you to lift up those who are suffering physically, emotionally, or spiritually, asking God to bring His restorative touch into their lives.

It is important to seek God's guidance as you pray. Each community and situation has unique needs, and God can reveal to you how you can specifically intercede on their behalf. You can ask Him to give you wisdom, clarity, and sensitivity as you lift up those in need. The Holy Spirit can guide your prayers and show you where your efforts can make the most impact.

While you may not always see immediate results or

understand the full extent of your prayers' impact, you can trust that God hears us. In Matthew 7:7, Jesus encourages us, saying, "Ask and it will be given to you; seek and you will find; knock and the door will be opened to you." your prayers are not in vain. God is attentive to your cries, and He responds in His perfect timing and according to His perfect will.

As you pray for the world, remember that prayer is not a passive act but a call to action. Your prayers should be accompanied by a willingness to be part of the solution. You can be the hands and feet of Jesus, actively working to bring about the answers to your prayers. Praying for justice means advocating for the oppressed. Praying for peace means seeking reconciliation and understanding. Praying for healing means extending compassion and support to those who are hurting.

Prayer is a powerful means of impacting the world. Through prayer, you connect with God's heart and intercede for the needs of others and the world at large. You can pray for peace, justice, healing, and transformation, knowing that your prayers are heard by a loving and faithful God. Commit to daily prayer, seeking God's guidance, and trusting in His power to bring about real change as you partner with Him in impacting the world through your prayers.

Section 7: Building Bridges

In a world filled with division and conflict, God calls you

to be bridge-builders. The Bible teaches you the importance of seeking unity and reconciliation among people. In Ephesians 4:3, it says, "Make every effort to keep the unity of the Spirit through the bond of peace." As followers of Christ, you have a responsibility to promote love, acceptance, and understanding.

To build bridges, you need to start by seeking to understand different perspectives. Instead of judging others based on their background, race, or beliefs, you should approach them with an open heart and mind. Proverbs 18:2 reminds us, "A fool finds no pleasure in understanding but delights in airing their own opinions." So be willing to listen, learn, and empathize with others.

Engaging in respectful dialogue is another crucial aspect of bridge-building. Instead of engaging in heated arguments or trying to prove your point, you should strive to have respectful conversations. James 1:19 encourages us, "Everyone should be quick to listen, slow to speak, and slow to become angry." By truly listening to others and valuing their opinions, you can create an atmosphere of respect and mutual understanding.

Promoting unity and reconciliation is at the heart of building bridges. Galatians 3:28 reminds us, "There is neither Jew nor Gentile, neither slave nor free, nor is there male and female, for you are all one in Christ Jesus." Regardless of your differences, you are all part of the same human family. You should actively seek opportunities to bring people together, fostering an environment of harmony and cooperation.

Love and acceptance are key in building bridges. Jesus teaches you in Matthew 22:39, "Love your neighbor as yourself." By showing love to others, regardless of their background or beliefs, you demonstrate the transformative power of Christ's love in your lives. You should strive to build connections with people who are different from us, extending kindness, respect, and compassion.

Building bridges is not always easy. It requires patience, humility, and a willingness to let go of preconceived notions. However, the impact of bridge-building is far-reaching. It can mend broken relationships, heal wounds, and create a more harmonious and impactful world.

Remember the example of Jesus, who crossed cultural, social, and religious barriers to reach out to people with love and grace. He broke down walls and brought unity. As His followers, you are called to do the same.

Building bridges is a vital part of your Christian journey. By seeking to understand others, engaging in respectful dialogue, promoting unity, and demonstrating love and acceptance, you can be bridge-builders in a divided world. Embrace the calling to build bridges, knowing that through your efforts, you can contribute to a more peaceful, compassionate, and impactful society.

Section 8: Embracing Global Perspectives

As followers of Christ, it is important for you to embrace global perspectives and understand the challenges faced by people in different parts of the world. In the Bible, Jesus teaches you to love your neighbors as yourself , and this includes your global neighbors. Acts 1:8 reminds you that you are called to be His witnesses not just in your local community, but to the ends of the earth.

To embrace global perspectives, you can start by educating yourself about different cultures, traditions, and ways of life. The Bible tells you in Romans 12:2 to not conform to the patterns of this world, but to be transformed by the renewing of your minds. By learning about the diverse world God created, you gain a deeper appreciation for His creativity and the beauty of His creation.

Developing empathy and understanding is also crucial. The book of Proverbs encourages you to seek wisdom and understanding, and this includes understanding the experiences and struggles of others. You can read books, watch documentaries, or engage in conversations with people from different backgrounds to broaden your understanding.

In the story of the Good Samaritan (Luke 10:25-37), Jesus teaches you about the importance of showing compassion to those who are different from us. The Samaritan, despite the cultural and religious differences, extended love, and care to a stranger in need. You can follow his example by reaching out to those in need around the world, whether through supporting charitable organizations, participating in mission trips, or advocating for justice and equality.

As you embrace global perspectives, you become global citizens who seek to make a positive impact on a global scale. The Great Commission in Matthew 28:19-20 calls you to go and make disciples of all nations. This means not only sharing the message of Christ's love in your local communities but also reaching out to the farthest corners of the world.

Remember, embracing global perspectives is not just about helping others but also about receiving blessings and growing in your faith. As you engage with people from different cultures, you gain new insights, learn from their faith journeys, and experience the richness of God's diverse kingdom.

Open your heart and mind to embrace global perspectives. May you seek to understand and love your global neighbors, knowing that your actions, no matter how small, can have a ripple effect of positive change across the world. Together, impact the world for God's glory and share His love with people from every nation, tribe, and tongue.

Section 9: Advocating for Justice

Advocating for justice is a crucial part of making a positive impact on the world. God's Word calls you to stand up for what is right and speak out against injustice. In the Bible, you see numerous examples of individuals who fought for justice and defended the rights of the oppressed.

Proverbs 31:8-9 says, "Speak up for those who cannot speak for themselves, for the rights of all who are destitute. Speak up and judge fairly; defend the rights of the poor and needy." These verses remind you of your responsibility to be a voice for the voiceless and to fight against the mistreatment of others.

Jesus Himself demonstrated a deep concern for justice. In Luke 4:18-19, He declared, "The Spirit of the Lord is on me because he has anointed me to proclaim good news to the poor. He has sent me to proclaim freedom for the prisoners and recovery of sight for the blind, to set the oppressed free, to proclaim the year of the Lord's favor." Jesus actively sought to bring justice to those who were marginalized and oppressed.

As advocates for justice, you can raise awareness about social issues that plague your world. You can educate yourself and others about poverty, inequality, human rights violations, and environmental concerns. By understanding the root causes of these problems, you can better address them and work towards finding solutions.

Supporting organizations and initiatives that promote justice is another way to make a difference. Whether it's donating to charities, volunteering your time, or using your skills to contribute to relevant causes, every effort counts. You can join forces with like-minded individuals to bring about systemic change and create a fairer and more equitable world.

Advocating for justice also requires you to examine your own life and make choices that align with God's principles. You can strive to treat others with fairness, kindness, and respect, regardless of their background or circumstances. By living justly, yourself , you become a positive example and inspire others to do the same.

In your pursuit of justice, it's important to remember that ultimately, it is God who brings true justice. Isaiah 61:8 assures us, "For I, the Lord, love justice; I hate robbery and wrongdoing. In my faithfulness I will reward my people and make an everlasting covenant with them." you can find comfort in knowing that God is on the side of justice and will one day make all things right.

Advocate for justice, following the example of Jesus and guided by God's Word. By speaking up, defending the rights of the oppressed, and supporting initiatives that promote justice, you can contribute to a world that reflects God's love, fairness, and compassion. Together, strive to make a lasting impact and alleviate the suffering of others.

Section 10: Mentoring and Investing in Others

Mentoring and investing in others is a biblical concept that holds great significance. The Bible teaches you the value of passing down wisdom and investing in the next generation. In the book of Proverbs, it says, "Listen to advice and accept instruction, that you may gain wisdom in the future"

(Proverbs 19:20). This verse emphasizes the importance of learning from those who have gone before you and sharing that wisdom with others.

Jesus Himself modeled the act of investing in others through His discipleship. He selected twelve disciples and spent time teaching and mentoring them. He imparted His knowledge, wisdom, and life lessons to them, empowering them to continue His work. Jesus said to His disciples, "Go therefore and make disciples of all nations, baptizing them in the name of the Father and of the Son and of the Holy Spirit" (Matthew 28:19). This command emphasizes the significance of mentoring and investing in others, passing down the teachings and principles of the faith.

As believers, you are called to follow this example and invest in the lives of others. You can mentor and support those who are younger or less experienced, sharing your knowledge and life lessons. By doing so, you empower them to discover their own God-given mission and talents. In the book of Titus, Paul encourages Titus, saying, "Older men are to be sober-minded, dignified, self-controlled, sound in faith, in love, and in steadfastness" (Titus 2:2). This verse highlights the responsibility of older individuals to mentor and guide the younger generation.

Investing in others goes beyond just sharing knowledge and wisdom. It involves building relationships, offering guidance, and providing support. It means being a listening ear, offering encouragement, and praying for those you invest in. By investing in others, you have the opportunity to shape their lives and leave a lasting impact.

When you invest in others, you multiply your impact. The knowledge and wisdom you share have the potential to be passed down through generations, creating a legacy that continues to shape the world. It is a way of living out the commandment to love your neighbors as yourself (Mark 12:31). By investing in others, you contribute to their personal growth, help them discover their purpose, and equip them to impact the world in their own unique way.

Mentoring and investing in others is a vital part of impacting the world. By sharing your knowledge, wisdom, and life lessons, you empower others to discover their God-given mission and talents. Drawing inspiration from biblical teachings and the example of Jesus, you understand the significance of investing in the next generation. Embrace the opportunity to mentor and support others, building relationships, and leaving a lasting legacy that continues to shape the world for years to come.

Wrap Up

Impacting the world is not reserved for a select few but is a calling for every believer. Embrace your God-given mission by serving others, sharing God's love, and leading by example. Use your skills, talents, and resources to make a positive difference. Pray for the world, build bridges, and advocate for justice. Mentor and invest in others, practice stewardship, and persevere in faith. As you step into your God-given mission, you become a catalyst for change, bringing hope, healing, and transformation to a world in need. Remember, you have the power to impact the world.

Impacting the world begins with recognizing your potential and embracing your God-given mission. Serve others, share God's love, lead by example, and use your skills and talents to make a positive difference. Pray for the needs of the world and actively work towards unity and reconciliation. Remember, even the smallest actions can have a significant impact. Step into your God-given mission with courage and conviction and watch as you contribute to a world that reflects God's love and transforms lives. You have the power to make a difference.

DR. SCOTT SILVERII

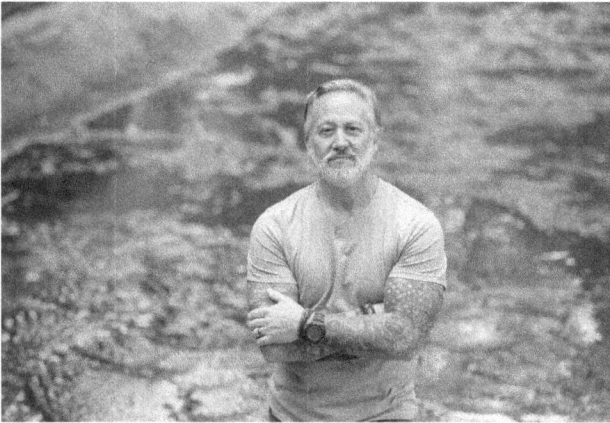

Dr. Scott Silverii is a son of the Living God. Thankful for the gift of his wife, Leah, they share seven kids, a French bulldog named Bacon.

A highly decorated, twenty-five-year law enforcement career promptly ended in retirement when God called Scott out of public service and into HIS service. The "Chief" admits that leading people to Christ is more exciting than the twelve years he spent undercover, sixteen years in SWAT, and five years as chief of police combined.

Scott has earned post-doctoral hours in a Doctor of Ministry degree in addition to a Master of Public Administration and a Ph.D. in Cultural Anthropology. Education and experience allow for a deeper understanding in ministering to the wounded, as he worked to break free from his own past pain and abuse.

ALSO BY SCOTT SILVERII

Favored Not Forgotten: Embrace the Season, Thrive in Obscurity, Activate Your Purpose

Unbreakable: From Past Pain To Future Glory

Retrain Your Brain - Using Biblical Meditation To Purify Toxic Thoughts

God Made Man - Discovering Your Purpose and Living an Intentional Life

Captive No More - Freedom From Your Past of Pain, Shame and Guilt

Broken and Blue: A Policeman's Guide To Health, Hope, and Healing

Life After Divorce: Finding Light In Life's Darkest Season

Police Organization and Culture: Navigating Law Enforcement in Today's Hostile Environment

The ABCs of Marriage: Devotional and Coloring Book

Love's Letters (A Collection of Timeless Relationship Advice from Today's Hottest Marriage Experts)

40 Days to a Better Military Marriage

40 Days to a Better Corrections Officer Marriage

40 Days to a Better 911 Dispatcher Marriage

40 Days to a Better Police Marriage

PAY IT FORWARD

•Watch your other Bros 6!

　•Share this book with other warriors.

　•Leave a review online wherever you bought this book.

　•Post the book and buy links on your social media so others find the help they need.

　•Message me for interviews, speaking, blog tour or questions. Personal email - scottsilverii@gmail.com

　•Be the Warrior God created you to be!

www.ingramcontent.com/pod-product-compliance
Lightning Source LLC
Chambersburg PA
CBHW071432090426
42737CB00011B/1634